Will

Wallace

Scotland's Hero

PRO·LIBERTATE

A biographical essay

BY THE SAME AUTHOR

Poetry
Makers and Destroyers
Love's Troublesome Journey
The Sex Doctor
Scotland's Saint
Wrong Ticket Home
Surveying the Wreckage
Likabehandlingsplan: Sweden Considered in Verse

Education Series
The Belt Room
Curriculum for Excellence
Queens of the Reich
Relentless: The Death March to Educational Excellence

Biography
Robert the Bruce
Janet: A Life in Verse

Free ebooks
Let's Go Ahead, Then!
Epiphany in Azure: Columba on Iona

Check www.glenntelfer.me for current and future titles.

William Wallace

Glenn Telfer

Certain that someone out there likes this stuff.

Published By
Big Ride
6/3 Pinkhill Park
Edinburgh EH12 7FA
Scotland

A catalogue record for this book is available
from the British Library.

ISBN: 978-1-909297-22-7

Cover art by Tim Pomeroy

Design by Wordsense Ltd, Edinburgh

Printed and bound by CPI Group (UK) Ltd,
Croydon, CR10 8YY

CONTENTS

	Page
Introduction	1
Scotland Then	5
Young Days	13
The Great Cause	23
Invasion and Conquest	33
Wallace Arrives	43
A Tough Man	49
The Scottish Nobles and the English	59
The Battle of Stirling Bridge	73
Into England	91
In Power	97
The Battle of Falkirk	107
After Falkirk	117
Wallace Abroad	125
The Hard Year	139
Our Man	149
Author's Note on Sources	155

William Wallace

Scotland's Hero

His name, who Scotia's fetters broke,
Shall never lose its power to charm,
Who liv'd to shield her—dying spoke
The weakness of her spoiler's arm.

John Jamieson 1820

A biographical essay

INTRODUCTION

William Wallace; a brave heart in a noble cause.

———————◆·————————

The phrase 'Cometh the hour, cometh the man' could almost have been coined with Wallace in mind; an unconnected figure who steps out from anonymity to rescue his country from extinction while others dithered, and who tragically died in this eventually successful cause. This is a universal hero story whose attraction needs no justification. But for us in Scotland, we also find that it is in his story that we first see ourselves clearly in history as Scots; identified as such and self-identifying so. And, too, in our own age of guile and empty talk among our leaders, we sense somebody that spoke and acted simply and only for his country. Whatever Wallace did, he did it for his country, for Scotland. His Scotland is not exactly our Scotland, of course, but it is in most ways that matter.

Wallace has no story separate from the story of Scotland's long fight to retain her independence from England. We know nothing of his interests and private life, indeed, from the time that we first know of him he can scarcely have had any. His story rushes with detail blurring speed from drawing his sword in front of the Sheriff of Lanark to his execution at Smithfield 8 years later, with a few brief stops along the way for battles at Stirling and Falkirk. This absence of facts brings serious problems for a factual essay like this one. The facts cannot speak for themselves.

However, we are not left with nothing. Our knowledge of the period considered in specific context can bolster the necessary speculation. Further, as we are absolutely unchanged in our basic psychology from our medieval ancestors, so can their mind-set be reasonably imagined. And Wallace, as a man, can be understood as being constituted and motivated like any other. Indeed, his personal weaknesses as a man and as a leader are the necessary backdrop to his actions which make them heroic. The fear, the doubt, the small voice overcome again and again, are what makes the hero. Where there are no frailties or fears there is no humanity, and we enter the realms of fantasy, or psychopathy. Wallace's flaws need not be denied, and indeed it is their presence that makes his achievement great. This is my operating principle for this story.

Wallace's story raises an issue with perspective: In our age we seldom, if ever, encounter someone with the massive physical and probable spiritual presence of Wallace; how should we present such an unknown character? When we consider the extreme events of his life and bloodthirsty morality of his age, with which Wallace must have been in tune, we realise that his story can be presented in a number of different ways, not all of them flattering to Wallace. I state this as a caveat and accept it as a challenge.

In hard times he was a hard man. But whatever the rights and wrongs of the events, his country was invaded and badly treated. There was no recourse to legal complaint or political action, the only remede was war. These were not wars of technology, but direct face to face violence. Hardness wins here. His bloody morality is a given for his age and Wallace's actions must be seen in this light. He was not claiming himself as a saint with a message of peace, there is no hypocrisy about him. Whatever the shading of our view of him, rosy or dark, he must above all be considered as a man of his time.

We must imagine him as a plain speaking man and perhaps one whom we might think had little time for the faint-hearts and schemers in the Scottish camp. But he must also have been a realist who knew that life's choices are seldom simple things, and this must have tempered a hard-hearted attitude. He would have understood directly through his own extended family situation, the tricky position that many had been placed in by the war. And especially the noble families, whose sense of honour and compromised loyalties were especially acute. He must have sympathised; at least, at first.

However, wars are not won by sympathy and fence-sitting. It needs someone to step forward, see things simply and take the leadership. Someone to put himself on the line and invite others to do the same; to represent, in person, the principle of a free Scotland all the way through to the bloody end. This was Wallace. I have come to understand him as a particular type of man, flawed and incomplete like any other, but born for that moment in his country's history. And, as such, the very definition of a hero. This is my view and bias.

The War of Independence was a long time ago, but many of its themes still resonate: The Scots' distinctiveness as a people, their relationship with England, the strong hold our sad past still has on our deep feelings; all these are things not yet resolved. We look to the past, to the lives of men and women who lived in that old Scotland, to find some answers. Of course, there aren't any as such. But sometimes, in all this thinking, you can get a sense of how the various virtues that can be seen in those times; courage, loyalty, perseverance and faith, still have a noble role to play in our country's future. It's a sacrifice that comes down to us today. All our past acclaims our future.

Rebel and martyr, soldier and icon; Wallace's story has many meanings. I explore the one I understand as true.

Glenn Telfer,

Edinburgh, December 2018

SCOTLAND THEN

**Our country, a magical and vast land with God's
stamp of freedom marked all over it.**

————◆————

Most of the world's countries are comparative
newcomers. Some, though, can be found far back in
time. Scotland is one such country. A thousand years ago
something closely resembling her can be seen clearly,
both in a geographic sense and in the minds of her
people. But Scotland did not appear in a snap of a finger.
No, it took a lot of pain, truces and treachery, hard hearts,
courage, and most of all, decent and hard-working people
to bring Scotland into being.

For numberless centuries, generation upon generation
had struggled to win a living from the land. It was this
never-ending cycle of daily graft that built Scotland out
of the hard wilderness that was so much of our country.
And it was this same day to day toughness that more
often than not kept the land out of the hands of greedy or
desperate people from other places. Sweat and tears, the
swing of a sword and spilt blood were the midwives of
Scotland's birth.

Right from the beginning of our history as a country, before our story of Wallace, Scots found themselves jammed between bigger and unruly neighbours. There were the axe-wielding Vikings, only a boat ride over the North Sea, always on the look-out for land and slaves and booty. The Irish were not far away; cousins, it is true, but already well noted for being unpredictable and ready for a fight. Finally, there was England. We were bad neighbours and found it hard to just leave each other alone. Although, at the time our story starts there had been no proper war between the two countries within living memory, it was common knowledge that every English prince harboured ambitions to win Scotland somehow, and fulfil an ancient legend by becoming King of Britain.

In the 15th century, Blind Harry the poet would phrase this ambition thus:

> *It has beyne seyne in thir tymys bywent.*
> *Our ald ennemys cummyn of Saxonys blud,*
> *That nevyr yeit to Scotland wald do gud.* *

The uncertainty and violent danger that often surrounded life in these olden times obliged the Scots to be always ready to defend themselves and their own. While necessary, this perhaps made them more prickly and weapon loving than was ideal. For inevitably this mind-set leads people to turn on each other, and feuds and ugly rivalries were common. But it also made the Scots

---

* It has been seen in past times, That our old enemies of Saxon blood, Have never yet done good to Scotland.

no soft touch; if their land was not held fiercely, it would be fiercely taken. The thistle, truly a most apt symbol for Scotland.

In this age before careers and savings and the security of the state, the land itself was the only true thing of value. It was the people's only larder and they were always on it. Working with it, or against it, forcing a living from it or dying in the attempt. It was their source of pride or misery. Their love of the land and sense of connection to it has no modern equivalent. They were the land and the land was them. This land called Scotland.

In Wallace's age, what was that country like? What would be our impression if we went back? The first thing we would notice is how quiet it was. The birds, the wind, the beasts, these would be the sound of outdoors. Occasionally, a ringing bell or the clang of the blacksmith's hammer. You would notice the freshness of the air, the reek of peat fires, the rich and heavy smell of cattle; provided, of course, you were not near the latrine pit or the midden! Scotland was a land of small settlements of farmers and keepers of sheep and small cattle, perhaps in number something over a quarter of a million. There were some towns and some big castles and churches, but much of Scotland was a land of empty space; wild and lonely mountains and moors, lochs and woods and great forests. In these wild places lived deer, boars, wolves and, so people believed, spirits, goblins and fairies; some good, some bad. It must have seemed a bigger place then, certainly more mysterious and magical. Scotland was, as it still is, beautiful.

But Scotland was also a hard land. Our ancestors had to work very hard indeed to survive. It was dangerous too. Disease and starvation were never far away, and always near their thoughts. Wolves still roamed at will. Robbers could strike at any time. All the years of back-breaking toil would count for nothing if illness came or the crops failed or your sheep were stolen. Because of this ever-present sense of impending disaster, people had a strong sense of fate forcing itself on them. But accompanying this sense was a greater ability to endure whatever hardship came, or the self-sufficiency to tackle it head on. The land and the weather made them physically tough and resourceful. It made them a proud people too, for everything they had, they deserved. Especially their freedom.

Freedom, this 'noble thing', to quote our 14th century poet, Barbour, appears early in our story of Wallace and is present in every page, whether clearly stated or subtle as a watermark. Everyone loves it, but few can define it, far less keep it. It is one of these human universals, like love or justice, that shape shift and slip through your fingers, and all the more so the harder you try to describe and grasp it. We have heard much of freedom recently, and perhaps seen how it is a partner and apologist to tyranny of some sort. There never was an age of freedom, and the freedom our medieval ancestors enjoyed appears to us as a very limited and provisional thing; it was. As is ours. The English conquest of Scotland did not replace freedom with tyranny, but it did suddenly introduce new hardships and insults. Even if the practical consequences of the invading army and the following imposed administration levelled out over time, one would still be left with the insult. And it is here, in the realm of the imagination, that freedom finds its fertile soil. In Wallace's story it becomes a catch-all for all the disappointments that would be put right with the expulsion of the English. We will not know if Wallace and the Scots patriots expressed their desire for the old king restored, the enemy expelled and their 'ancient privileges' once again enjoyed, as freedom. Barbour, mentioned above, Bruce's medieval biographer, brings the mention of freedom into this story, and it has stuck since. Our cause, the war of independence, has become the very definition of a struggle for freedom, whatever it means and whatever our ancestors thought it meant. Perhaps, for them, like us now, they sort of knew what they meant by it and that's enough definition. Philosophers can delve into the specifics, the relativity, and the absurdity of the idea, but the ordinary mind needs a banner with a simple message. Freedom does that job. This is what we mean in this story whenever freedom is mentioned.

Freedom might have the same loose meaning for us and them, but other things not. As their world was different, physical and hard with few possessions and even less luxuries, so too their notions of what was useful or interesting must have been different from ours. They were not schooled as we are, few could read or write, and certainly none of the peasantry who made up most of the population. Consequently, their knowledge of life in other places was sketchy or fanciful; the English race having tails like monkeys, for example. Most people lived their lives within the circle of the community they were born in. This perhaps tended to make them narrow and isolated in their thinking and world of reference. But this gave them a depth to their thinking in that small world of field and hamlet and market. They knew about the land, having words for features that our modern eyes would not recognise. They knew about soil and seasons. They knew about wood and stone and working them with tools. They knew about the ways of the beasts that they worked. They were interested in stories of their ancestors and, just like us, the affairs of their masters, friends and families. Things that confused them, we can now explain with science. But, on the other hand, things that confuse us they would see clearly as the work of heaven or hell. They could be just as sensible and just as daft as us. We must remember that we are talking about real people. Sometimes, in imagining the past, modern authors (like this one) create lists of ancient qualities that can make our ancestors' lives, as they lived it, seem like a simple thing. And they themselves, simple people. This is not intended. These people were not naive or any more credulous than us, they had the same rational powers of interest and understanding as ourselves. The sum total of their learning easily matches ours, although comprised quite differently. The sum complexity of their life was the same as ours, although generally much more precarious.

Perhaps, the greatest difference between us and them is that they believed in God and his will. They believed it with a depth and sincerity long lost to us. Their faith was the source of so much of their strength of character and amazing fortitude. They felt the benevolent presence of God in all that they did. It was this faith that gave meaning to their lives and to their deaths. And they were a people who knew how to die.

Wallace's Scotland was a feudal society, like England and the rest of Europe. But, when we get to the specifics of the feudal system as it applied to Scotland, we find that it was not like England at all. Scotland never had its entire ruling class replaced at a stroke, as occurred in England after William the Conqueror's victory at Hastings in 1066. This created an ethnic as well as culture rift between society's leaders and the common folk which took centuries to level out and create a common sense of Englishness. Scotland's feudalism was a gentler process (for want of a better description) which mixed and matched to the local conditions, creating a kind of hybrid feudalism, that had a strong tribal or clan character inherited from a Celtic past. This preserved the linkage between society's many social layers, it might not always have been gentle and understanding, but it was there. The feudal elite, many with their Norman ancestry, were integrated with the various native elites, to create a Scotto-Norman elite. This talk of a common sense of Scottishness that link top and bottom in Wallace's Scotland is not intended to obscure or deny the very real and strictly enforced social divisions, but it meant that there was a common bond whose continuity linked everyone to the land and its history. This had a socially levelling effect and Scotland's elites were never quite the remote figures of their English counterparts. This was to be of great significance in the coming wars of independence and especially in Wallace's story.

So much has changed since the time of Wallace's story. This can make us believe that people then were so different from us. But they were not. We have their eyes, their faces, their hair, their smiles and laughter, and their temper and sad faces. They were, as Scots still are, a people made by the land and the weather and history. Looking back over seven hundred years, we can still see ourselves in them and them in us. Us, their children.

When it happened, the English invasion of Scotland was so terrible an event that most people were too afraid to do anything. But there were others who, afraid though they would be, thought that their duty to their land and families and country was a precious, even sacred, responsibility and could not be ignored. They are the ones who said 'No' to foreign conquest and the injustices following it. It is these people who give life to our story. Such a person was William Wallace.

YOUNG DAYS

Just a lad, special in his own way, like any other.

William Wallace was born around the year 1270 probably in Elderslie, near Paisley. He had two older brothers, Malcolm and John, and probably two sisters.

As indicated by their surname's original meaning, foreigner and/or Welsh, the Wallace family may have at least partly been able to trace some origin in the immigration to Scotland of families connected with the feudalisation of Scotland beginning in the late 11th century and consolidated in the early 12th. But too, the name was applied to people from the old, and by our Wallace's time, long gone ancient Kingdom of Strathclyde, who originally spoke Brythonic, an extinct Celtic language (the original British tongue) related to Welsh. Given his family's proximity to the regions which once spoke Brythonic, this is the most likely origin of our Wallace's background.

The Wallaces were quite well off, having land in Ayrshire and Renfrewshire. Their relatives had land all over Lowland Scotland, and possibly all the way up to the North-East. There is uncertainty about Wallace's father's name, Sir Malcolm Wallace having the longest pedigree, but it could have been Sir Alan; Wallace's probable Seal of Office when he was Guardian suggests the latter (*Filius Alani* – son of Alan), although the seal is damaged and it is not really clear. Although, Wallace's father had a title and was a knight, he was not part of the nobility. This is a very important distinction as it marks him (and his family) as excluded from the great offices of power.

And this completes what we know for certain about Wallace's early days and family. As previously noted, almost everything else comes from Harry's *Wallace*, which we cannot accept as a fact. Of course, as with any fiction, there is always the possibility that some of it has echoes of real life.

However, the absence of solid facts does not mean that we are left with nothing, for we can make some good assumptions about Wallace's upbringing based on our knowledge of the Scotland of his time. We are all creatures of our age, few of us step outside these limits, except exceptionally and briefly; in this truth we can find something of Wallace. Compared to a modern biography, with its vast archives of documents and letters and photos, we may find ourselves disappointed at the vagueness inherent in this requirement, but we must remember that any historical figure, as we understand them, is a creation of the imagination and none more so than national heroes. Wallace is a man, as such he would have been no different from any other in his essential nature. Of course, the differences from 'your average man' are great, but even here he must have shared the same basic psychology as other great leaders and warriors from history.

The important thing about Wallace's story is not to be culled from archives. What he was like, what made him tick, is to be found within ourselves. This phenomenon has long been recognised. The biographer establishes the facts and the context, but we make the leap in empathy to proper understanding. In Wallace's story, this leap has to be a bit longer to make up for the deficit in facts. Your sense, then, of the man and leader behind the bare bones of the story is dependent on your own imaginative and emotional capacities. And too, the ability to search out meaningful comparisons in your own study of personality through books and movies, and your own life. Understanding Wallace's story, I suggest, becomes a kind of self-journey, his biography and your own biography feeding off and informing each other.

In Wallace's day few people had any schooling as we would understand it. And it is probably only in the study for a life in the church that we would recognise anything that would look like a school lesson. And it would be under the church's auspices that, whether intended for a church career or not, the few who could read and write would learn this skill. This would be taught in Latin, the common language of books, documents and letters then. We must remember, though, that this skill does not necessarily equate with speaking it well.

If we cannot know about Wallace's schooling, we still can fill in broad details of his early learning and this is probably a better way to think of his education; rather than importing into our thinking modern school and college based ideas of classes and tests and educational levels. Society didn't learn like that then.

Young Wallace would have learned of his family history, and all the stories of his ancestors and fellow countrymen that had won the land and its freedom. Of course, coming from a family of landowners, or more properly land-holders (holding the land for service and rent from their tenant-in-chief, their baronial overlord), he would have grown up very aware of their dynasties and connections to other similar landowning families. And especially, their connection to the land in both a legal and ancestral sense. This link to the land, their land, was a very powerful force in their lives. It was a link to their ancestors who had won it, probably with the sword. This creates a powerful blood responsibility. As we have alluded to earlier, there is a spiritual as well as practical dimension to this which, as urbanites, we cannot fully appreciate. But this would be in Wallace's bones.

He would have learned about the bible and prayers and the place of the Christian faith in life. Sitting uneasily with this Christian knowledge was the belief in a pre-Christian spirit world of fairies and goblins and other unlikely creatures; in the empty and dark world after sunset, these beliefs would be easy to hold. He may have been sent, as was a habit in the extended families in those days, to stay with relatives, not as a holiday (although perhaps that too) but as a way of learning other skills and good manners and how to get on with people outside one's immediate family. Basically, one was a servant or worker, although still a family member. This was the way that families, spread out across the whole country, as Wallace's was, maintained their strength of connection. This could help with learning other languages, or at least different dialects.

Story telling, poetry and music were the main forms of entertainment, and the ability to sing well and recite really long poems was highly regarded. Great powers of memory were required to do this well, as no notes were available to help. Indeed, almost all learning in those days was memory dependent.

Certainly, he would have been taught practical things connected with his family's position as landowners; things to do with managing an estate, animals, tenants. One thing we can be sure that he enjoyed learning was the martial arts; the use of sword and shield, spear and the dirk, bow and arrow. I can imagine him doing some extra 'lessons' without needing any encouragement. Not just as a little boy playing soldiers as we may today, but as an older boy deliberately practising these skills with focus. Perhaps the bow was an especially favoured weapon for him, as his Seal of Office referred to above shows a bow and arrow design.

Wallace would probably have grown up speaking three languages; Scots, Gaelic and French. The old version of the Scots language was the main language of Lowland Scotland in his day, but enough Gaelic might still have been spoken to make knowing the two languages commonplace. Gaelic might also have been the first language of some of the extended Wallace family who lived in the north. French was the first, or first equal, language of much of the nobility, as it was in England too, and anybody with connections to the nobility, someone like Wallace's father, would speak it of necessity. Wallace would have spoken Scots as his first language, which although an English language, was already distinct from the English spoken in England, excepting the northern border counties. Perhaps he spoke the other languages almost as well. Perhaps, if he had had some schooling, he spoke some Latin too. We shall never know.

Compared with our own times, in those days a person's job prospects were limited. Usually severely so. What you could do mostly depended on what your family did. In a family such as Wallace's, the titles and estates went mainly to the oldest son. The younger siblings were expected to make the most of what they had by hard work, enterprise or good marriages. As a younger (perhaps youngest) son of a fairly well-off family, Wallace would not necessarily have had great prospects ahead, but he could be fairly certain of some degree of security. Traditionally, sons like William went into military service or the church, and often both. This may well have been his intended future. Blind Harry mentions this. He has young Wallace educated by uncles who were priests, firstly at Dunipace, near Stirling, then later at Dundee. It is unlikely that Harry actually knew this as a fact, he was probably just making a common sense assumption and building a narrative around this.

Harry makes Wallace's early education by priests the source of his love of country. The priests inspiring the same by stirring patriotic tales. Certainly, the Scottish Church then was fiercely patriotic and politicised, this stance not only a consequence of earlier wars, but of the church's long-standing struggle for self-control against claims of over-lordship (and control of revenues) by the church in England. However, Wallace's love of his country need not have this exclusive source. Your feelings about your country are always some sort of combination of family and community attitudes, mixed with your education, and then something personal in how you understand your place and purpose in life.

Scotland then was a very tribal sort of place; identity was family based and local, ordered around the great estates of the nobility and their retainers and tenants. Scots were strongly aware of the distinctions in speech and allegiances between themselves and other Scots, in some places these distinctions shaded into feud. But Scots too were aware of the common bond that united them. That of shared hardship and history, of loyalty to their king and their land. This bond came from a distant Celtic past and was first given name and shape by the Romans and their walls. Then later forged in warfare with the Irish, Vikings,

Angles and English, and not least among themselves, giving the country its present boundaries and warlike mentality. Later still, refined by the Celtic church with its love of the land and finally by the Roman church with its order and European sensibility and connections. This bond was greater than all the differences; at least, most of the time. By the time of King Alexander, if not before, Scots increasingly thought of themselves as Scots, replacing earlier and now archaic ethnic identities of Picts, Britons, Danes, Norwegians, English and Gaels.

It must have been this sense of the common bond that Wallace was exposed to as a youngster. And not just him. From the grandest to the poorest, noble to cowherd, man and woman, wherever they came from, Scotland's ancestors were to show that Wallace was not unique in his feeling for his country. It was not then, as it is not now, a simple thing. But it was real.

What else can we assume about young Wallace from this historical perspective? Probably nothing significant. But, as we know the man, so do we know the boy. Sturdy, adventurous, a lover of action, proud (perhaps too much so), headstrong (definitely too much so), brave, honest, willing. We can imagine him being rather too determined for his own good at times. We can never know if he was an especially thoughtful or reflective man, how deep down his gentler nature lay, how light-hearted or witty he was. All these other human sides to his personality have been lost to the warrior we know of. But they must have been there. It is a shame for our history that this other

Wallace is unknown and ignored in his story's telling, for it creates the impression by its absence of a hard and inflexible man. This he undoubtedly was, but only surely in those areas of action that required it.

Wallace may indeed have been considered for the priesthood at one time and, as we have seen, this need not rest on Harry's claim. However, he seems an unlikely person for a priest, perhaps his parents realised this and cut off that option. If so, for us in Scotland, we have to recognise the prescience of that decision and be grateful for it.

THE GREAT CAUSE

**Scotland and England; two countries at peace
with each other, but brought to war by accident
and ambition.**

Trouble can often arrive out of nowhere. And this is how
our story begins. Prior to the tragic events that were to
mark the beginning of our woes, Scotland had been a
peaceful and prospering country for a whole generation.
Then, one bad black stormy March night in 1286, the king,
Alexander III, reckless to win home to the arms of his new
bride, Yolande of Dreux, accidentally rode his horse over
the cliffs at Kinghorn in Fife. The weather that night, a
harbinger of the storms to come.

Medieval monarchs were not the symbolic personages
they are now. They were the working head of state
and government, personally involved in all important
decisions; all authority flowed from them. As such, they
were the ring that held the disparate parts of the land
together; the human embodiment of their country. They
were identified with and revered, or feared and rejected,
to an extent unknowable to us now. Perhaps some sense,
although from a later age, of this spiritual and symbolic

significance of the king can be felt quoting Shakespeare's *King Henry V*:

> Upon the king! let us our lives,
> Our souls, our debts, our careful wives,
> Our children and our sins, lay on the king!

And Alexander was a loved monarch who was rightly credited with Scotland's stability.

His reign and death would be remembered in the lovely opening verses of Andrew of Wyntoun's famous *Oryginale Cronykil* of Scotland from *c.*1420:

> Quhen Alexander oure kynge wes dede,
> That Scotland lede in lauche and le,
> Away was sons of alle and brede,
> Of wyne and wax, of gamyn and gle.
> Oure gold was changit into lede.
> Christ, born in virgynyte,
> Succoure Scotland, and ramede,
> That stade is in perplexite.

> *When Alexander, our king, died*
> *That led Scotland with laughter and love*
> *Away went abundance of ale and bread*
> *Of wine, increasing prosperity, of fun and games*
> *Our gold was turned into lead*
> *Christ, born of a virgin*
> *Rescue Scotland and give a remedy*
> *For we are in trouble.*

However, in this case, the tragedy of a popular king's death went beyond the usual woe. For Alexander had no direct offspring to inherit his throne. Queen Yolande, however, was pregnant with the king's child; this would save the crown and Scotland should a, hopefully male, heir be born. Alas, continuing the woes, Yolande miscarried or perhaps had a stillbirth. Her personal tragedy amplified the national one. Was civil war in the offing now?

The only direct claimant was the king's three year old grand-daughter, Margaret (named for her mother, Alexander's daughter, who died in childbirth), who was the daughter of King Eric of Norway and thus a Norwegian princess too. Following Alexander's earlier instructions, she became Queen of Scots, although she is usually known as the Maid of Norway in Scottish history. As a little girl still in another land, the country was ruled in her name by a group of appointed nobles and churchmen known as The Guardians. This was the legitimate and accepted method of running a country while the monarch was a child. Given that we know the importance of the monarch's direct role in government, we can appreciate that their absence, as in this case, creates the potential for jealousies and nepotism within the governing Guardians. The threat of civil war or invasion always hung over countries in this situation. Scotland would feel this tension and, indeed, in this period, mutual suspicions led to some aggressive manoeuvring which brought Scotland to the very edge of civil war.

There was a crucial issue surrounding the management of the little queen's future; who should she marry. Whatever king could arrange such a match for their son would win a stake in Scotland, and possibly, eventually, win Scotland herself through this connection. Marriage arrangements for infants were a common part of international diplomacy, and completely separated from the personal feelings of those involved. Part of the Guardians' role was to ensure that whatever match was made was done so in the best interests of the country and its young queen. Naturally, King Eric of Norway was keen to see his daughter's future tied to a strong (and useful) match and had already made overtures to, at least, King Edward of England; this being done independently of the Guardians. King Edward too was, naturally, already interested. These were two kings whose interests would have to be accommodated. Scotland, after all, lay between those realms. There was a possibility of the Guardians being outmanoeuvred by these other kingdoms in arranging the little queen's fate. This awareness must have acted as a spur to action.

Probably the best deal was reached when a treaty was made in July 1290, the Treaty of Birgham, arranging for King Edward's son to marry Margaret. In some hard bargaining, the English king had tried to get the Scottish negotiators to surrender certain Scottish rights and laws, thus reviving the old English claim to suzerainty, although disguised as a legal requirement, but this they had refused to do. King Edward was probably not too concerned about this, as it was something that could be resolved later after the marriage. But first, Margaret had to be brought back from Norway.

Disaster! 26th September, 1290; due to some unknown infection, the little queen died en route to Scotland. King

Edward's hopes, and perhaps ambitions, for Scotland were dashed with this news. The tragedy went beyond this little girl's death. The Scots themselves were in a great quandary; what to do, who would be king? It was not clear to the Guardians how this would be resolved properly and fairly. And all the old suspicions and rivalries returned when the various claims to the throne were considered.

There were a number of claimants for the empty throne, but Robert Bruce and John Balliol, two of Scotland's most powerful nobles, were the main contenders. Each had a genuinely strong case and many supporters who correctly felt that they had much to gain or lose depending. In this time of warriors this situation was a tense one, everyone it seemed kept their hand near their sword hilt. Choosing the merits of the different claims ultimately rested on which criteria were adopted for comparing them. Who would or could do this without prejudice, and without antagonising the losers and their supporters? It seemed no one.

Scotland appeared to be sliding into civil war. It was at this point the Bishop of Saint Andrew's, Scotland's senior cleric, wrote to King Edward of England asking him to solve this problem by judging the claims and deciding by law which was best. It is not known if the bishop's letter was the result of a collective decision to do this, or some other initiative, perhaps even knowingly going against opinions that had reservations over the wisdom of this act. However, it was not without logic.

King Edward was among the most powerful kings in Europe, his word had binding authority. He was also our kingly, and still yet friendly, neighbour with a legitimate interest in the outcome, and recent involvement due to the royal wedding negotiations. In a sense, to not solicit his opinion or good will might have been viewed as disrespectful. This was a serious consideration; any who had met him knew him as a powerful presence that should not be crossed. He also had, in common with most medieval kings, an informed interest in the law, especially as it related to landowning and titles and inheritance. This dispute over regnal primacy would only be peacefully solved by such an informed appreciation of the weight to be given to the various documents and evidences. King Edward could provide this. In any case, whatever considerations and reservation surrounded his involvement, once he was involved there was no going back on it. The king agreed to participate and a civil war was avoided.

It is at this point in our story that English and Scottish historians often disagree. English historians have tended to present the king's intentions and actions as honest. The concessions he required consistent with his role as judge, and his dignity as King of England. Scottish historians have taken the opposite view. They have felt that from his beginning of the process his behaviour was essentially diplomatic bullying with the deliberate intention of eventually creating the situation that actually arose; one that would allow him to legitimately step into some dispute or disorder as peacemaker, and would end with him as Scotland's master. When we consider some of the world's recent conflicts we can see that such manoeuvrings are equally well known in our own age.

We have already noted how much governance then was focussed on the person of the king, and thus in considering him we can come to an understanding that perhaps reconciles the English and Scottish opinions. A king's role was to protect his kingdom and extend it if possible. This was not just their job, it was their sacred duty and, indeed, whole purpose to their life. Kings were obsessively aware of the burden of history as it flowed through them to the future. A future in which they wished to be remembered as just and strong, bequeathing to their descendants a stable and prosperous kingdom. And enlarged, if possible. The 'if possible' is the issue here. King Edward was aware of the future possibilities inherent in his undertaking to act as arbiter in the Scottish succession. He was well aware of claims by earlier English kings to over-lordship over the Scottish kings; claims that had slipped back somewhat. He was aware of ancient prophecies that predicted one great king for the whole of Britain, might this be him? And why not? He was aware of his reputation as a warrior king and a conqueror (of Wales), a reputation that, in that age of wars, was much respected by his own people. Even if unspoken, King Edward would be subject to these background pressures which required him to maximize the possibilities for England. His own people would expect this. His sense of his own dignity would require this too. But the king was not a tyrant, he wished to, and to be seen to, follow procedure and the law. I believe that these two counter-currents ran around his mind during the succession process. In a sense, as we often find in our own lives, he probably did not really know his own mind and how the psychological burdens we have mentioned were working on him. I am not meaning to impugn his intellect, which was powerful, but just to make a general point that often one is not aware of their own mind's workings.

The selection process, known as The Great Cause, was a vast diplomatic and legal undertaking. And it started off ugly; the Scots suspicious, the English king frustrated. In setting out the conditions which authorised him to judge the claimants, King Edward insisted that it was necessary for the Scots to surrender aspects of their country's sovereignty to him and for the contenders to owe him fealty, in other words, recognise him as their legal master. How could he arbitrate, the argument went, if those to be judged did not recognise his authority over them? This was the old over-lordship issue returning. The Scots rejected this at first, Edward was, after all a foreign king who had no right to make demands of the subjects of another monarch. Moreover, the counter argument went, he could still pass a legal judgement independently of fealties. Even ignorant of the then law in this regard, as we now are, we can still easily realise how legally tricky these propositions were. But you have no monarch, Edward would argue, and so to whose authority in this process do you submit, if not me? And if me, then recognise this in the accepted manner by an act of fealty. The king insisted on this and, contender by contender, eventually got his way. Any dissent now did not matter. Once the king insisted on this concession, it is difficult to see how he could be denied it and still be expected to arbitrate. Many Scots must have realised that this was going to happen and perhaps too the eventual consequences for their country. For these prescient Cassandras and canny neutrals, this whole process must have been like living the nightmare.

The Great Cause was a lengthy process, taking well over a year. And, except for the absence of women as participants, remarkably modern looking in its bureaucratic thoroughness. As it dragged on and surely got heated, as the secret deals were done, as the pressure rose, so the king's essential personality would increasingly become the dominant factor. King Edward was an intelligent man, but not an intellectual type, nor remembered for his patience and gentleness. I think, then, that he came to lose patience with much of the debate. And possibly too, with all the scheming and dealing, respect for many of the participants. He would have perfectly understood that many of the claimants were not serious contenders, but there to cut themselves a deal with the big players. They could easily be seen as time wasters and schemers and, as such, unnecessarily delaying the outcome. As this happened so the king's attitude would harden and he would find himself playing a manipulating game too. The pretence gradually slips away, and cynicism shows its face. To return to our original point then, regarding the king's intentions, during the succession debate; I contend that there were two stages. The first part where he believed that he was impartial, and while obviously not unaware of his own interests in the outcome believed that he had fairly neutralised them. Then a second stage, starting some months into the process with King Edward now frustrated, self-interest consciously comes into play. And scheming is, of course, infectious. From optimism to cynicism; many negotiations in our own time, in our own private life even, follow this pattern.

The Great Cause is fascinating. It well rewards the effort to explore it, by revealing a thoroughly modern mix of principles, wheeler-dealing and cynicism which provides, I believe, a route into understanding that the mind-set of our ancestors was exactly the same as our own; an understanding we can profitably apply to the rest of our story. Right now, though, we must return to our main narrative and leave the Great Cause with a decision, after 16 months, finally reached in November, 1292. John Balliol, Lord of Galloway became John the First, King of Scots.

By the criteria adopted this was a fair decision. As expected, it was not universally popular, but it was accepted. The new king was crowned at Scone, as per tradition, and then, as demanded by his overlord, went to Newcastle to swear his oath of fealty to King Edward. Scotland's king was now a sub-king. King Alexander had been deftly able to resist this 'right' in his whole 37 year reign, King John's reign starts with surrendering it.

INVASION AND CONQUEST

People then, as now, were touchy about their national identity. Sensitive to distinctions with neighbouring lands and especially so on issues connected to national honour and respect.

———◆———

The act of fealty was just such a thing that touched this raw nerve. There is something demeaning and diminishing about it, no matter how necessary and legal. Throughout the middle ages kings always had a problem with having to swear this oath to other kings, even for minor territories held in another king's land. Ordinary Scots would have felt the same. National identity was focussed on the person of the monarch and the oath would have been seen as a new development bringing them down a notch. And against England, too! Although probably understanding of King John's position here, he was still the king who swore it and who physically by this act made their country the lesser land. It's a situation pregnant with future trouble.

They didn't have to wait long before it turned up. King Edward took his overlord status very seriously and to the letter; interfering in court and church decisions, hearing Scottish legal appeals and in various small ways showing who was boss king. King John must have felt the indignity of this and been aware that he was starting to look like a puppet. But what could he do; he had sworn an act of fealty and King Edward was merely enforcing it, as was his right. There seems almost a studied cruelty to King Edward's diligence in this respect. He well understood its implications for the Scottish king. It seems as if he considered King John as 'his man.'

Now, King Edward at this time was preparing for a war with France. This was over the confiscation of his Duchy of Gascony by his overlord for these lands, the King of France; ironically, in many respects the result of a similar situation as was occurring with King John! The king instructed King John that he wanted military help from Scotland, as was his right as overlord. Scotland had no quarrel with France and there was no desire to become involved; partly on principle and partly for the obvious fallout for those Scots nobles (like King John himself) whose French estates would be confiscated by the French king and whose extended families and interests would be compromised. This was the crisis contained in the Great Cause finally arriving.

The debates in the Scottish government must have been intense, the danger in every option chosen obvious. Being logical, the best option would have been to go through the motions of following King Edward's demands, or otherwise ineffectually supporting him just enough to keep it legal with the oath. King Edward would have seen through this approach, and so such a solution could only be regarded as an expedient. But it would probably have been enough to avoid outright and immediate censure by Edward. And a lasting displeasure from the French king. With luck, such stalling might last long enough to see the crisis otherwise resolved. And then some serious (though insincere) grovelling from the Scots would have fixed the diplomatic insults to both French and English. However, this pretence would have hurt the Scots' pride.

The actual Scots' response of refusing the English king and immediately making a defence treaty with France, the start of our Auld Alliance, shows the strength of frustration in Scotland at King Edward's behaviour. The Scots knew the English king well enough to know that, although distracted by war in France, he would not take this lying down. Scotland prepared for war. The nightmare feared since King Alexander's death had become real. Of course, as there always is, some men would welcome the nightmare.

King Edward found out about the Scots' treaty with France and prepared to teach the Scots their final lesson as an independent country. As part of the defence deal the Scots invaded the north of England, hoping, before the English forces were fully mobilised, to win some success and also relieve pressure on the French. The Scots campaign was no doubt cruel, but militarily ineffective, and the main army had retreated back to Scotland by the time King Edward arrived personally to lead the invasion. He started it at Berwick, then a thriving seaport and one of Scotland's biggest and wealthiest towns. The town refused to surrender and then resisted his assault, and following the custom of the day, the following successful assault led to its destruction and the massacre of its civilian inhabitants, possibly to the number of thousands. King Edward was not a man bothered by the better angels of his nature when crossed. The war had started ugly.

News of the atrocity fired the Scots. Revenge was on their minds. The chance came very soon as King Edward advanced further into Scotland. At Dunbar, on April 27th, 1296, the Scottish army attempted to lift the siege on Dunbar Castle and met a detached part of the English army. They let their hearts rule their minds and so flew into the English who were advancing on them. The charge and skirmish style of battle favoured by the Scots was something the more experienced English had seen before while fighting the Welsh and Irish. It did not panic them. They maintained their formations, repulsed the charge and broke the Scots with a counter-attack. The Scots fled in disarray. Those horsed escaping with their life. Scattered foot soldiers would have been ridden down and killed, perhaps some were allowed to surrender. Some Scottish knights and significant supporters of King John were captured. As battles go, it was small scale and the casualties low even for the defeated Scots. However, although not destroyed, the Scottish army had been humiliated and taught a hard lesson about the quality of their foe. Those wavering about what to do now didn't need it repeated. Many of King John's supporters abandoned him. Those who were originally his opponents in the Great Cause having already done so, our Robert the Bruce's father, for example.

King John fled northwards, but more to buy time and come to accept the reality of his lost kingdom, than with any serious thought of further resistance. The English king's pursuit had more the flavour of a leisurely procession around a new acquisition, than a chase. He already knew the inevitable ending to King John's story. King John too finally accepted the inevitable and surrendered and formally abdicated in early July, 1296 at Stracathro in Angus. This took the form of a humiliating ceremony conducted partly on his knees before his master, King Edward. The ceremony was repeated a number of times in other locations to ensure Scots got the message. The humiliation was not just for ex King John, as the personification of his country it would be felt by all. Less than four years after helping judge for their king, Edward was their king. To his soldier companions the king joked, *A man does a good job when he rids himself of a shite!*

One cannot help thinking that, not only was the inconvenience of the king's campaign in Scotland more than compensated for by the terrific success he had enjoyed at low cost, but there was an inevitability about it all. King Edward must have enjoyed immensely what seemed like a fated neatness in his fortune.

---

* *Bon bosoigne fait qy de merde se deliver!* Should you ever find the need to repeat the same in Old French.

The king made the necessary arrangements to run Scotland as a conquered country using trusted and proven administrators and military men. His experience of conquering Wales and incorporating it into England had given him the practical knowledge of how to do this. Of course, he could expect support from connected Scots too; as the vast majority, around 1800 of the major landowners, had sworn a new oath, recognising his authority, in the so-called Ragman Rolls, as the document has subsequently been called. They had, of course, no real choice in this.

The king returned home a conqueror, bringing with him the deposed king and other booty as fitted his fancy. Included in the war gains was the famous 'Stone of Destiny' which was to find its new resting place on a shelf under the king's throne in the Palace of Westminster. As the stone was integral to the crowning of Scottish kings, its symbolic significance was immense. Whenever King Edward sat on his throne he sat on the Scots. As a hardened soldier with a sometimes crude turn of phrase, the vulgar possibilities are many.

Poor King John: At this range in time, the judgements of history are simple and emphatic things. We will never know what kind of man John was or, whether circumstances being different, he may have made a good king. The key to reputation and affection for a monarch is longevity. King John failed in dramatic fashion, the gavel comes down to pronounce; loser. Only we, if we are so inclined, may find some sympathy for him and accept that there was a personality behind the enigma left to us. But one fact, made massive by its absence, reveals itself; King John lacked the resolve and sense of destiny we find in the great kings. The moment, when it came, crushed him. Perhaps he came to his kingship a little too late in life, being in his forties, and too unexpectedly, to adapt to the role. Perhaps, winning the throne by legal process damaged his legitimacy, above all to himself.

Returning home, his conqueror, King Edward, probably expected some trouble from Scotland, but he would have been confident of being able to handle it. His experience of managing rebellion in Wales had given him insight and operational knowledge. Militarily, he knew Scots rebels would not be able to match his own soldiers in battle. Meanwhile, he had the issue of war with France to attend to.

With the English king back in England and the ex Scottish king, with his son and erstwhile heir (14 year old, Edward), in comfortable confinement in the Tower of London, let us consider Wallace again. Tales can be found regarding his whereabouts during this period. However, the lack of records are emphatic; we just don't know. It seems reasonable to guess that he would have wanted to fight and so could have been at the Battle of Dunbar and took part in the shameful retreat following it. Equally, he may have been elsewhere with other elements of the Scottish army. Either way, with the disintegration of Scottish military resistance in the face of King Edward's procession through Scotland, he was disbanded, or more likely disbanded himself. It would not be difficult to believe that he felt shamed and angry, and had set his heart against accommodation to the new order. It must have felt to him that Scotland had been lost too easily. Many Scots felt like this. But what to do?

It was obvious that conventional warfare was not an option. The English were too powerful. And the Scots nobles, whatever their private feelings, could not be relied on; this factor, at a stroke, decapitated the usual leadership in war. And too, denied the legitimacy that flowed from their involvement, as well as the obvious supplies and safe bases that they could provide. It is very easy to bring down a hard judgement on the Scots nobles, perhaps seeing them as cowardly or selfish; and many have taken this view over the centuries, from the comfort of their safe homes. But the nobles' situation deserves some consideration and sympathy.

Firstly, they had sworn a solemn oath to King Edward; an oath that legally, if unfairly, recognised and accepted the king's rights in Scotland, and the legitimacy of the situation as it now was. To go against this was to risk more than just their principles, and even their life. Their entire family could be utterly ruined, even destroyed. Their estates, titles and privileges, built up carefully perhaps over centuries, all gone forever. The risk didn't just end with their immediate family. The extended family, retainers and tenants could all pay with their livelihoods and lives; for war then was no respecter of innocence when it visited. Especially for traitors, as the Scots nobles would be considered. Besides, who could lead such a rebellion? Scotland's king was now an ex king in exile in London.

Resistance to English rule would have to come from people whose duty to their country was not just clear to them, but uncomplicated by circumstances such as we have just described; typically, young men, like Wallace. They would immediately be considered as criminals and outlaws by the English. They would be hunted and if caught, undoubtedly executed. This would be no war of grand knights and waving banners, it would be an outlaw's war. Ugly, deceitful, wasteful, like all wars; but much more personal. And in your face, or more likely, back!

King Edward had barely left Scotland when resistance to the new rule sprung up. Patriots or opportunists, freedom fighters or brigands, brave or cowardly, principled or fanatic, just or cruel; views along the spectrum that are as valid then as now.

WALLACE ARRIVES

Scotland needed a hero to inspire and unite it.

Sir William de Haselrig was the English appointed Sheriff of Lanark. It was with men like him that the English ran the country. He was unlikely to have been the evil figure of Scottish legend, but he would certainly have been ruthless; this was not an age that was lenient on those who broke the king's peace. The Scots would have hated and feared him. The troops he commanded and the justice that he dispensed were the most obvious symbols of English rule. He would have known how he was regarded and would have been, understandably, a bit paranoid.

The 3rd May 1297, the day of the finding of the Holy Cross (following the style of medieval date recording), was also the date for the county court in Lanark. And on the day, or perhaps night, Wallace and his companions slew Sheriff Haselrig and his staff. Haselrig then, apparently, cut into collops. This was a major blow against English domination and the first time we have proof of Wallace in history. The town would have been in uproar. Outraged and afraid the English and their Scottish supporters could see that the rebellion had taken a new turn for the worse.

Away from English eyes, a few celebrations would have been the order of the day.

How this was done we do not know. Blind Harry's poem has Wallace seeking revenge for the murder of Mirren Bradefute, his wife or wife-to-be, by Haselrig's men. He has the sheriff's assassination taking place in the middle of the night. After killing the guards, Wallace smashes in Haselrig's door.

What's going on? Who is it?, Haselrig cried out.

Wallace, our hero shouted, *The man you're looking for!*

You can feel the grue running up Haselrig's back at hearing these words. He tried to escape into the darkness, but his time had come. A sword swing split his head to collar bone and he was dragged downstairs to be dirked just to make sure. His house was then put to the torch.

Can you imagine the scene in the streets that night? In the darkness; burning buildings, horses panicking, dogs barking, groups of men with torches and bloody weapons, curses, cries and screaming. *What's happening! What's happening!*

All this is fanciful, of course. But it conveys something of the boldness and violence of the deed. What it misses is the planning side. The sheriff knew he would be a marked man and would have had a permanent bodyguard. It would not be possible to just rush in and kill him. It is frustrating to know that the details of this significant event in our story is lost to us. Only its occurrence is confirmed as a fact in the charge sheet from Wallace's trial. Perhaps a sense of the options for this deed can be found in recent history, where a more powerful country has invaded another and set up a government whose legitimacy is not completely accepted by the conquered people. Here we know that behind any attack or outrage are often networks of spies, traitors, double-agents, the bribed and threatened. This would have been part of the background in the story of Haselrig's murder. His death, perhaps planned for months.

In this age long before guns, and especially explosives, guerrilla warfare and terror type activities, like assassinations, needed very careful planning to maintain the advantage of surprise. Firepower could not make up for any deficit in numbers between opposing forces, and it would do the Scots cause no good to just fight the English man for man. Operations would have to be planned to give the enemy no chance, easier said than done. The intelligence needed to do this would have to be matched at the cutting edge, so to speak, with an extreme boldness. You would have to make your heart cruel, for killing then, with sword and spear and dirk, was a very personal business. You have to go right up to your opponent, and if it goes wrong, then your only option is to fight your way out. Or die; your death a cruel, messy thing, like that you had planned for your victim.

Up to this point the rebellion would have been presented by the king's officers as the actions of leaderless soldiers and bands of thieves. And while not entirely untrue, everyone would have known that the reality was different from this. However, it would be important (as it still is, as we regularly see today) to deny rebels any legitimacy. King Edward, with his experience of the same type of events following his Welsh war of conquest, would have understood all this well. However, the murder of the sheriff, a political act, is concrete proof of the rebel's motivations. They were challenging the king's authority. This fictional view of the rebels as brigands could not be held anymore. Brigands and thieves don't do things like this for fear of the reaction it would provoke from the authorities. The rebels wanted this reaction. And so, this was now a rebellion proper.

However, Wallace was not the only one causing trouble. There were similar actions over most of central and eastern Scotland. By the time of the sheriff's murder it was clear that the country had not settled down to accept the new order and that, in fact, there was a country-wide rebellion. Outside of the castles and fortified towns, Scotland was not a safe place for anyone connected to English rule.

At first the various rebel groups must have been small, but this would in no wise impede them becoming a powerful focus for hope or fear, recruitment or annihilation. At first, they would have acted independently and in their own areas, although probably loosely aware of each other's activities. Fairly quickly, however, they must have collaborated and increasingly consolidated into larger groupings, of possibly up to a few hundred, as required by the operational requirement of any particular action. Certainly, by the time of Haselrig's murder, it seemed to the English authorities that there was a mastermind behind it. In an age before the rapid and various communications we now take as necessary, and when so many were illiterate, there was only one possible source with the connections and ability to coordinate and advise the rebels; the church.

The English authorities were in no doubt as to the ultimate source of the problem; the Scottish Church. There is much truth in this. The support of the church was crucial to the rebellion. Indeed, as an institution, the church's hostility to English rule could be considered as a rebellion in its own right; a spiritual template of resistance that inspired others whose sphere of action was in the secular world. With many nobles unsure what to do, it was the church that conferred legitimacy and, with its country-wide network of parishes, could act as an intelligence system. It is impossible to exaggerate the importance of this support to men and women then. A support that goes beyond the practical we have spoken of. For theirs was an age whose belief in their religion was as yet unchallenged by rival ideas or made redundant by plenty. There was a simpleness to their belief, and their church commanded respect and had authority. Without the church's role, perhaps the rebels would indeed have ended up being brigands or malcontents. The rebels' strength flowed from the certainty of the church's blessing. The church was the rebel's rock. And the anchor that fastened the rebellion to the rock was Robert Wishart, our Bishop of Glasgow. If there was, as the English saw it, a mastermind behind the rebellion. He was it. We will return to this great patriot later in the story.

It is also clear that the rebellion was not the creation of the Scottish Church, although English authorities presented it as so. The real source of the rebellion was to be found in the hearts of men and women all over Scotland. You ask yourself; do you care about this? The answer determines the future.

A TOUGH MAN

That sword swing against Haselrig made Wallace Scotland's most wanted outlaw and its natural leader.

In the early days of the rebellion with all its suspicions and disorder and confusion people look to find someone strong and certain in their actions and their outlook. The people need a leader that looks and acts like one. They want an action man. And when found, the people make themselves believe that this person is more and better than they actually are. This new-found leader becomes a symbol of their hope. An instant hero. This happened to Wallace. Suddenly he has the glamour of great power and the welcome (and unwelcome) attention that comes with fame. But hidden in this to all, even to the wise, is a self-corrupting force. Mastering this negative force is always the greatest challenge the hero faces.

But what made the killing of the sheriff so important? We have to understand this to understand why Wallace became Scotland's hope and leader.

Sheriff Haselrig would not have been the first of the king's officers, supporters or troops to be attacked and killed.

But the others, in the scheme of things, were nameless and trivial figures. His subjects and servants, true; but people who could be replaced. The king would have been concerned at news of this, of course, but probably not too much.

The sheriff, however, was in a completely different category. He was a representative of the king; this meant that he was the very symbol of the king and his justice in the actual absence of the king himself. The sheriffs also were personally appointed by the king, this direct link gave them much of his royal authority. In addition, the sheriff's job was vastly more important and powerful than its modern equivalent. If we think of a judge, police chief, military commander, local government Head of Service and ambassador all rolled into one job we get the idea of the sheriff's position. However, there is no simple modern comparison with a medieval sheriff's job that allows us to understand, the way people then did, the enormity of the sheriff's killing. This is something people then knew would hurt the king's dignity, and that King Edward would take this very personally.

Scotland now has an outlaw killer of one of the invading king's representatives. And Wallace now tops the king's Wanted List. Rewards for his capture (dead or alive) would have been offered and punishments for giving him succour threatened. Wallace is the hero Scotland is waiting for. Can he live up to this? What is his next trick?

We only have Blind Harry, alas, to turn to for tales of Wallace during this period. He has Wallace, inspired directly by the divine agency of a visionary 'qweyne' (*Welcum*, scho said, *I cheis thee as my luff*) to correct the 'mekill wrang'* his people have suffered. Even Saint Andrew (Saynct Androw) turns up to give a sword.

And then, assisted by his close friends, Gray, Kerlie and Stephen of Ireland, avenging insults and meeting the challenge of English strongmen and sword champions. The English and traitorous Scots are hacked down at every opportunity. Women, children and priests are the only folk of 'English blood' who are spared the blade. Harry even has Wallace fighting a lion for the French king and comparing doing so to killing a dog.

The real stories would have been long remembered in tales and songs, but they have not made it to our time. These stories would be less dramatic than Blind Harry's, although hardly less cruel.

There is a difference, though, between bold and reckless. The Wallace of Blind Harry's tale is too easily ruled by fiery emotions, too reckless to lead men well. The hard and canny survivor that was the real Wallace would not have risked his own and his followers' lives in the way that Blind Harry's poem tells. This Wallace truly is a fictional leader.

---

* Translation: queen, great wrong

Also, these real stories properly viewed, would reveal something else that is generally missing from heroic tales. Something that is paradoxically revealed by the absence of reference, and that is the everyday courage of the rebel's life; the need to live with physical hardship, psychological tension and the boredom of camp life. The need to do the difficult organisational things, the planning debates, the making of compromising concessions that was essential to a rising leader in Wallace's position. All these things that challenge your faith in your own ability and the rightness of your choices; and thus reveal its strength.

The real Wallace became the leader because he lived up to the challenge it posed. And others recognised this when they saw it. In an age in which leadership was literally from the front, Wallace would have had to be first in physical courage, toughness and audacity. He would have needed weapons skill and prowess. He would have needed a military mind and intelligence. He would have needed ruthlessness. But one more thing. He would have needed strength of spirit.

Many, possibly most, of the qualities we have described could be applied to any number of brigands and hard men. But these men don't and can't lead armies. Wallace did. He was able to attract followers for his deeds, but only keep them because of his spiritual qualities. This is what his followers recognised, even if they didn't always know it. This is what they were seeking in their leader. Having no established command structure to step into and work his way up, in order to lead his men Wallace would have to have charisma and natural authority. He so obviously *was* the leader. The brave warrior is a given, but it is spirit that makes the hero. This is a quality that lives in the eyes and needs to be viewed first hand for it to work. In crucial ways this style of leadership is the exact opposite of the manufactured celebrity cult and audience manipulation that characterise national leadership in our own days. He was the epitome of leadership, literally, from the front. All men seek this in their leaders. In our own age we only find it figuratively.

Danger and hardship were the rebels' constant companions. Cold Scottish rain running down the back of your neck, cold winds, cold damp leather, cold wet feet, a frosty morning's wakening with stiff bones on the hard earth. The fireless camp with only a stone to suck to hold back the rumble of your belly, the poor horses having only the hard iron of the bridle for their sustenance. The odd sound, or a crow's sudden flight, that makes your heart race and has you fitting an arrow to the bowstring. Hearing kind words and warning of danger from people, but at the same time searching their eyes for the traitor's smile.

There is no romance in this life inside a stinking suit of chain mail. Only the satisfaction of being true to your cause, your companions, yourself.

The hours in the saddle, the hours of watching and waiting, the terrible tension of the wait. And then, the whoosh, a rush of arrows. Ambush! Dirt and blood mixed freely. The dagger in the back, the slit throat, the lopped-off hand, the crack of bones, the face ruined forever, the sickening thud of an axe, the cross-bow bolt shot into the skull. Blood and more blood.

No opportunity was missed to punish the English and their supporters. Cut them down, burn their castles and homes, steal their money and supplies. Be called a coward and a murderer by your enemies and revel in the insult. You had to be hard for this sort of thing. Even in that hard age this was still an unusual calling. Wallace showed that he was the master of it.

However, although this was a hard age, this did not necessarily mean that people were harder hearted than they are now. Nor more cruel. But the type of war that the Scottish rebels were fighting, was by its very nature crueller than a war of battles. It was a type of war that would later be called guerrilla warfare or terrorism. It is much more personal and unfair and indiscriminate and it quickly hardens hearts on all sides. We have seen examples of this experience in our own recent wars, the comparisons can usefully inform our understanding of this period in our history.

In this feast of violence, English domination and Scottish resistance grew ever bigger by feasting off each other. Reprisals follow reprisals. The killing of one innocent person on one side is matched by the intentional same on the other. In this depraved chasing circle, the Scot and the Englishman proved themselves equals. There was no surrender, no prisoners were taken, except for interrogation. If you were caught, you would be expected to be given the chop. And probably you would be. Perhaps, some lucky few were kept for prisoner exchange. In any case, having a small force and no fixed base, the Scottish rebels certainly would be in no position to hold prisoners.

We are used to hearing of this type of war now. And it is obvious to us, as it was to some of our Scottish ancestors, that this small-scale guerrilla war was the only option available. The Scots had no answer to English military prowess on the battlefield, nor to their heavy cavalry, nor to the resources of their vastly wealthier country. To meet England on the battlefield was to invite another defeat. However, people don't always act on the obvious. They stick to traditions and their leaders' choices, to established ideas of the 'right way' of doing something. In warfare, at this time, this was a summer battle where the armies were led by the nobles. Wallace and the other rebels rejected this approach. Of course, they had to. But they still did. There was no Manual of Guerrilla Warfare that they could look up for advice.

We are surrounded by alternatives in life, but seldom see them when we should. It needs someone special to see the truth of a situation *and* act on it; and then persuade others to act on it too. And this break with tradition marks Wallace out as no ordinary man. It makes him a revolutionary in some ways. We will return later to this idea.

Wallace's force was not the only Scots rebels that were active at the time of the sheriff's killing. Indeed, by then the rebellion was being described by English commentators as country wide. 'Country wide', though, excluded, as it often does, the far highlands and western isles. Their sheer remoteness and insular culture made them almost like a separate country, and certainly generally outside of any royal writ. Their involvement in these events, both at this and later stages of this story, would always be relatively small. And dependent on each chief's personal considerations and sense of opportunity, rather than direct invasion or concern over regnal rights.

What this wide-scale rebellion actually consisted of must have varied from area to area, some places by their geography and politics, more suited to supporting (and hiding) rebel forces. And too, the various allegiances that complicated Scottish politics would play a massive role here. But although perhaps the majority of the population supported the rebels, the actual numbers of them must have been small. From a practical viewpoint, and especially foddering horses in the winter months, Wallace could not have moved around with any more than a few hundred, and perhaps usually no more than a few score; a large band, certainly, but hardly an army. Joined together, all the rebels could make a formidable force, but how was this to happen? The sheriff's killing seems to have been the catalyst for this.

The rebellion got the boost it needed. Wallace became famous, the name people could now fix to the rebellion. Heroic leadership answers a deep human need and people flocked to join him. Soon he was leading a large body of rebels on horseback, bigger and bolder now, challenging the English authorities to oppose him. Indeed, Wallace with Sir William Douglas almost captured King Edward's most senior official, the Justiciar, William Ormsby, at his court in Scone. Ormsby escaped (just!) in time, but many of his entourage and his treasury contents did not. Other rebel groups in other parts of the country would have received a boost from hearing of these exploits. The common people, too, who had secretly supported the rebels could now do so openly, and this very act denied the country to its English managers and their Scottish supporters.

And then, sometime in early summer, Wallace joined up with Andrew Moray, who had been leading a similar rebellion in the North-East of Scotland. Roughly similar in age, the two men obviously hit it off. Their joint command, apparently, presenting no problem for themselves or their men. Together they made an army and this set about reconquering Scotland. In a very short time, English military forces were destroyed or routed in what must have been scores or even hundreds of minor actions. As the summer progressed, they increasingly found themselves insufficient to resist the Scots and either fled altogether or retreated with their various officials and supporters to the security of garrisoned castles. These were then sieged.

By the summer of 1297, excepting the town of Berwick and some castles, the English had lost control of Scotland. The country was being run by rebel committees. Scotland was Scotland again. But everyone would have understood how temporary this situation was. Scotland's natural leaders were still absent or quiet. The atmosphere was pregnant with possibility. The next move would have to come from King Edward. He may have been tied up with his affairs in France, but few would have doubted that he would find the time for Scotland. Or doubted his response.

THE SCOTTISH NOBLES AND THE ENGLISH

Many Scottish nobles supported the rebellion, but did so secretly for they feared the punishment of King Edward.

While Wallace and the other rebels were fighting most of Scotland's nobles had been quiet. The hard lesson they had been taught at the battle of Dunbar and its humiliating aftermath did not need repeated. As a group it is impossible to characterise them as a group. Every possible opinion about what had, and was happening, to Scotland would have been covered. Within families the same divisions existed, as we will see later when we consider the Bruce family. But what to do about this was the question?

Scotland's old king was deposed and they had a new overlord, however, all this was done with due legal process. Obviously, to say the least, powerful manipulation was involved; but, nevertheless, it was still done legally enough to compromise their conscience and make outright rejection of King Edward's regime an ethical and legal difficulty. And now, there was a rebellion which lacked a proper leader, as they would have seen it, from amongst their own ranks. What to do? Who exactly *was* this Wallace and what were his connections? How much could he be trusted? How were they to know in an age before records and information at your fingertips how to consider Wallace; brigand, opportunist, nutcase even! Was he a serious mistake in the offing? All they know is that he is not one of them. In a way, Scotland's nobles were still in collective shock at the sudden change which had yet to unravel and reveal exactly how each would fare in the new King Edward's Scotland. What to do when the risks are so great? One finds that in this situation most people wait and see what happens, play it clever, see how the land lies, 'Ca canny', to use the perfect Scots phrase for this approach.

Many supported the Scots rebels, but tentatively, provisionally and, above all, secretly. They were being watched. Not least by each other. Any support of any sort for the rebels would have to be subtle and deniable. Although they appear not to be part of the story at this stage, they must have been. They were the power in the land, their say counted.

Their attitude at this stage, if they were rebel supporters, would likely be displayed by what they did not do, rather than what they did. And that is, follow official instructions to hunt the rebels down, or otherwise aid the king's authorities to do so. They would not provide intelligence to the king's authorities. They would not prevent the rebels from obtaining succour, and perhaps arranging the same by proxy. Wait and see, let others with less to risk, as they would have seen it, take that risk.

Those who were more inclined to the new status quo, would also have found it prudent to adopt the 'wait and see' approach. Perhaps fulfilling their official duties to keep the king's peace with considerably less zeal than the king would have wished. We can see that 'plausible deniability', so well used in our own time, has an ancient pedigree.

The English authorities were certain that nobles were involved in the background as described above. This has sometimes been denied by later historians who view the Wallace led rebellion as entirely spontaneous and independent of noble involvement. Thus, the opinion of contemporary English commentators who have claimed noble involvement has been presented as a class prejudice, in that the medieval upper class who formed the governing elite could not conceive of a national rebellion that did involve their class as leaders. That the rebellion was populist and powered from below by Scotland's 'lesser men' and commons is undeniable. But this fact need not exclude the social elites from involvement. To deny them any role in this murky time is to fall, paradoxically, into the same class prejudice attributed to others. My take on this is simple; the English authorities at the time were not stupid, nor without insider knowledge. They knew how society worked, and so it is reasonable to accept their claim of treacherous noble duplicity as essentially true.

Wallace was not, however, a proxy for the nobles, or acting as the fall guy for their still hidden intentions. He was his own man and would not automatically defer to his putative social superiors. This must have been apparent to any who met him. But although he was a rebel, he was not a rebel to his own nation and its norms: or, at least, not intentionally. His fight primarily was to free his country from its invaders, but this was legitimised by the goal of restoring its rightful, deposed king, King John. There is a crucial difference here, which needs emphasising, between the rebel fighting for his country's honour and the radical championing a new social order. Wallace has often been identified with the latter; his early death and the absence of facts make it easy to politicise his actions and fit him up with anachronistic beliefs. And he has sometimes been viewed as a sort of medieval harbinger of the democratic and meritocratic Scotland most contemporary Scots embrace. However, although he could not be such a champion of future attitudes by intent, perhaps some recognition of the radical implications of his actions is revealed by the next move from the Scottish nobles.

They were no doubt impressed and inspired by the increasing successes of Wallace and Moray, maybe a little embarrassed too. But surely, also, afraid of being left out of their natural role as the country's leaders. Consider for a moment how this situation must have looked to their enemies, potential allies, Scotland's common people and, above all, to each other? Here we have a rebellion to restore Scotland's honour and rightful king led, not

by his nobles, but by a commoner! Also, if the rebellion
was successful, then those nobles who helped in this
cause would be in a commanding position; and the ones
who didn't, in a potentially ruinous one. And too, that
the rebellion was led by a social inferior, led by force of
personality, contained clear and unwelcome implications
whose radical aspect we have just referred to. It is not the
intention when referring to the calculated caution of the
Scottish nobles to impugn their honour or integrity. They
had the same stock of principles and pride as anyone else.
However, their wealth compromised the free exercise of
this, perhaps, by analogy, as our mortgage does today.
This is a fact simply made stronger as wealth increases,
for so does risk. For them, the risk was always potentially
catastrophic. There should, then, be no value judgement in
stating this limitation on their sphere of action.

As the rebellion picked up pace and the summer of
1297 approached, we find the Scottish nobles secretly
planning to betray King Edward and openly rebel. Taking
advantage of the breakdown in English control, the nobles
denounced their allegiance to King Edward's settlement
and assembled their own rebel army composed of their
followers and tenants. This secret planning and eventual
action being clear evidence of the nobles' essential
attitude to their country's fate and the Wallace/Moray
led rebellion. But, revealingly and crucially, they did not
join the on-going rebellion. Even those with family or
other strong connections to King John and who could be
thought of as natural allies to Wallace, preferred to keep
their rebellion exclusive.

The failure of the two rebel armies to join to the benefit of their cause has many historical and modern parallels. We have already mentioned how the social norms of the day would preclude the nobles from joining a common rebellion. The other way around is how it should be. In addition, such an act would permanently compromise the social privileges that class often enjoyed in warfare. To join the commoners was to invite the commoner's fate when things went wrong; instant death. No doubt a part of their collective thinking at this stage, even if unspoken, was to abandon Wallace if the right deal required this; *C'est guerre*, being the rationalisation!

From a logistic and practical point of view, keeping the rebel forces separate also made sense. In the absence of an overall leader, such as the king, commanding the various groups with their complicated relationships to each other was always going to be problematic. Wallace, of course, knew this and must have preferred the independence of thought and action which his independent command permitted. Only a naïve would surrender control of his faction to the snake pit of Scottish baronial politics. And Wallace does not seem a naïve.

The Scottish cause took a big leap forward with this second rebellion. Wallace and the already active rebels must have been pleased and not least because this legitimised further their rebellion. Surprisingly, perhaps, King Edward would also have been pleased. This sort of rebellion was the sort he could easily deal with. He could bring his army to meet their army. A battle, about whose outcome he was confident, would resolve the problem of Scotland. Those nobles who deep in their hearts opposed him would be destroyed. He probably realised that his victory the year before had been too easy, and this had had allowed his secret opponents to survive safe and hidden. Now they would be exposed and crushed. The other rebels like Wallace and Moray, if they survived, would be marginalised and the hidden support of noble supporters cut off. This would ensure, he would have figured, their eventual defeat.

The Scottish nobles met the English at Irvine.

But seeing once again their old conquerors returned, the fear of death was put into their hearts and they decided to negotiate instead of fighting. No doubt all their old divisions came to the fore once they actually had to decide what to do when the English turned up, no doubt the lack of a legitimate and authoritative leader hampered them, but still, their eventual decision was a pathetic one. On 7th July, they surrendered and once again pledged allegiance to King Edward. *Their* rebellion was over. Few battles are won so cheaply, and not a blister to show for it. For the hotheads in both camps this would have been a frustrating outcome. In this age a noble's reputation was often made on the battlefield, the outcome at Irvine clearly would not satisfy this need. From an English point of view this result made sense; they had proven themselves the better men, and avoided a costly and perhaps drawn out war. Especially important as the situation in France was King Edward's main concern. This is where he would want to focus his forces and to do so free from any complications and extra costs in Scotland. The surrender deal was part of his instructions and so the English negotiators could have felt that they had served their king well. However, privately as soldiers, they must have felt contempt. And frustration. They would have thought; *Why go to the bother of making an army if it is just going to surrender?* Survival over honour.

Wallace, no doubt, thought the same. He must have been excited at first by the nobles' rebellion, but the surrender, although a disappointment, could not have been a total surprise. He would have been aware of the divisions and discord in the nobles' camp and would have seen how it was going. Keeping his own force separate from the debacle at Irvine proving prescient.

Disappointments like this have the virtue of making things simple; it was clear now to Wallace, Moray and the other patriots that they could not rely on their country's so-called leaders to deliver their freedom. They would have to do it alone. For those who wished to join the patriots, well, it was clear now who to go to.

There was one benefit enjoyed by Wallace as a result of the surrender. The English forces were tied down while the negotiations continued. This left Wallace and Moray free to build and train their Scottish army in the forests of Selkirk free from interference and carry on with their campaign elsewhere. The English were in no doubt that the Scottish nobles deliberately strung out the surrender negotiations for this purpose. There is no reason not to believe this. As the negotiations got nearer to their obvious conclusion, probably a significant proportion of the nobles' own contingents slipped away to join Wallace, who was not, of course, included in any surrender deal. There is a certain recognition, and dignity even, in this exclusion which must have satisfied Wallace.

The people who joined Wallace and Moray that summer of 1297 owed their commanders no formal bond, but knew the justice of Scotland's cause and felt a strong sense of duty to their country. But it was Wallace's spirit that turned these feeling into action. And courage! It was his spirit that turned individual beliefs into a collective will that chose honour over safety. It is his spirit that turned our famously fractious ancestors into a coherent group that was willing to do the right thing. Scotland's pulse ran strong.

For Wallace to create and train an army that was prepared to fight against a formidable enemy at the same time as the country's normal leaders had abandoned that same fight was truly a great achievement. One that is too often skipped over, as we have no knowledge how it was actually done. And is thus often presented as a simple statement, as if such a happening was a commonplace and easily achieved. Consider, the essentially word of mouth nature of this organisational marvel.

Those turning up to join the rebels would have come with a range of military experience; farm boys and day labourers with none, many probably with some familiarity through their attachment to local militias, some with more dedicated skills, such as Wallace himself would have had. But, as Scotland had been essentially at peace with foreign neighbours for so long few could have had much experience of war, or even real fighting with weapons. Even when they had, it would have been limited to skirmishing.

The skirmish, essentially one-on-one style of combat, is almost an instinct; you select an opponent and attack them, or them you. After a certain level of competency has been taught, many of the essential skills for this way of fighting are very self-trainable. If one has the time you could spend the whole day at the bow butts on your own. With a companion (or even alone) one can practise shadow cut and parry with a sword. This combat style works well for self-defence, ambushes, raids and the various other small group encounters, such as the rebels had been involved in. However, this mind-set with its focus on individual prowess can be an impediment to fighting in much larger groups. Only large groups can resist cavalry and bring enough men to bear at a point to allow victory. Being brave and skilful in the use of weapons, in a one-on-one situation, is not the same as the ability to fight in disciplined units which can follow plans and instructions. This is what wins battles and this takes training for men and horses and leaders. Time and again throughout history men have found that bravery is not the essential ingredient in battle. The point of a battle is to arrange your army in such a way that you do not fight your enemy man to man, but overwhelm them at the point of contact. Achieving or avoiding this is what comprises good generalship. Training and standardisation of arms make this possible. And this, in turn, rests on logistics and camp discipline.

Men then generally led active outdoor lives and so hard labour and the privations of camp life would not have been a problem, however, they still need to be sheltered and victualed and controlled. And disciplined, they are not there to loaf about and bevvy, or come and go as they please. And above all, they need quality training. This leads us to another consideration too often overlooked; the planning of all this. The supply of standard arms and other equipment, the captains to lead the training, the lodging and camp arrangements for such a large body of men and, finally, the feeding of them; all this takes formidable logistics. All of which is invisible to us. It is not believable that this could have been accomplished without at the very least the tacit approval of the nobles and the support of the church as a major landowner and creator of food surplus. The church too, through bishops Wishart and Lamberton, supplying the funds here in Scotland and abroad for the various necessary victuals and fodder, munitions and bribes. So many in the background deserving of their place in history, but only considered, alas and inevitably, as footnotes to Wallace.

It is easy now to be hard on the nobles who surrendered at Irvine. To note, as a pointed criticism of them, that their first duty was to self and family and estate, is in all fairness just to note a commonplace throughout mankind. These 'biological' imperatives of self and family first are not separate qualities by which we measure the moral worth of our ancestors, but part of a wider set of identities and allegiances. As a class they did not lack courage or principle or patriotic feelings, but they lacked a leader. And this they needed more than anything else. Circumstances made Wallace free to follow his conscience, circumstances circumscribed the nobles' choices.

We know what the future was to be. At the time, all they could see was death staring them in the face. The English army at Irvine was tough and experienced. These English were not the 'carpet knights' who would be mocked in a later age, but the real deal iron men. The knights in particular, a powerful and crushing force of cavalry, to which the Scots had no answer. They knew, as we do not now, just how that difference in size and weight and quality of mount and armour translated to fighting power on the battlefield. They could see they were beaten already. In a way, after agreeing to negotiate, their surrender was their only viable option. Whatever you think of their behaviour, it would do their own cause, and wider Scots' cause, no good to be beaten. And it did help the cause by holding down the English forces while negotiating continued. Afterwards, no doubt, many 'surrendered' Scots went from Irvine to Selkirk to join the more resolute rebels under Wallace and Moray.

Intended or otherwise, it could be argued that the Scots nobles did a good job at Irvine of buying time for Wallace, and sewing discord and mistrust within the Englishcamp.

From the English point of view the surrender at Irvine brought benefits and problems simultaneously. They had won at no cost or casualties, which left their forces at full strength for tackling Wallace. However, in their coming campaign against Wallace they would have to factor in the unpredictable presence of the faced down, but undefeated and surely resentful, army of the Scots nobles. The deal struck hardly made them allies. They knew they had been played for fools, but it suited their purpose to preserve their force intact for Wallace. Once he was defeated, the other problems would become academic, the nobles would not revolt again.

There is no doubt that a complicated little game was played at Irvine. Obviously, no one trusted anyone.

THE BATTLE OF
STIRLING BRIDGE

**The English victory at Irvine was an empty one
for they did not regain control of the country,
nor had they addressed themselves to their
big problem – Wallace.**

By August 1297, Wallace had cleared Fife and Perthshire
of English rule. Now joined with Andrew Moray who had
liberated the north and east, he was besieging Dundee
Castle. All of Lowland Scotland, with the exception
of some castles and fortified towns, was under rebel
control. It was clear to the English that Wallace would
have to be beaten in battle or made to surrender. And it
had to be done soon. They had an army in Scotland, no
doubt itching for a fight after the frustrations of Irvine. A
thumping victory over upstart peasants would be just the
tonic to set them right. They marched towards Stirling
and towards Wallace and Moray.

Wallace and Moray's force marched to meet them. The
days of guerrilla fighting were over. It was time to take
their country back. And the only way to do this was to
destroy the basis of English authority, the army. It was a

risk, but a necessary one. Guerrilla warfare could make Scotland unmanageable from the English viewpoint, but as long as England could bring an army to Scotland they would always have the ability to retake the country. The English army must be destroyed, but was now the right time? From the Scottish rebels' point of view it was essential to establish their credibility with actual and potential supporters in Europe. The only way to prove that their claim of independence was worthy of support by foreign princes and bishops was to expel the English by force of arms. As so often in life, dispute comes down to force. The end destination of diplomacy, one group of men fighting another.

The 9th of September found the two armies at Stirling and both ready for a fight. At this point, some of the Scots nobles turned up and offered to negotiate some deal. This was a common occurrence before medieval battles, sometimes conducted seriously, but often one or both sides used it as manoeuvring to buy time, strike a dramatic posture and to psyche out the opponents. The Scots nobles would have been playing a very tricky psychological game here. Their hearts were with the rebels, but they had just surrendered to the English at Irvine and could hardly break that newly sworn bond. But they could not let their fellow countrymen be massacred, as they thought would happen. Using the same argument they had applied to themselves, it would do their long-term cause no good to have Wallace and his army snuffed out. We can imagine them saying so to Wallace and Moray; this was not the time and place for a battle. Let us wait and see what happens in France, let us wait until King Edward dies, let us wait on the Pope's judgement. Let us wait!

And all the time this discussion was going on, others were joining Wallace and Moray. The Scots nobles knew this was happening; and once again the delay in reaching an agreement was partly deliberate with this intention. The English commanders also knew, of course, what was going on here. You can imagine the collective groan and soldiers' curses filling the air (*Oh , for f... s....! Here they come again.*) as the Scots nobles rode up again to offer some other fresh 'deal'. One which they were bound by the conventions of the day to hear out. Here was the same procrastination and delaying tactics that they had experienced at Irvine. Enough of this nonsense, they would have thought! *Let's get a victory to take back to our king and shut up the ever double-dealing Scots nobles!*

One last chance to surrender was offered on the 11th September. Wallace's reply: *Tell your commander that we are not here to make peace, but to do battle and to defend ourselves and liberate our kingdom. Let them come on and we shall prove this in their very beards.*

So, it was to be a battle then. Good!

The two armies were separated by the River Forth. The English on the same side as the castle and the town which crowded around it. The Scots, ranged around the high ground now called Abbey Craig, where now sits the

Wallace Monument. They had around 5,000 men, the vast majority spearmen. Most would be relatively poorly armed and unarmoured, basically a local militia. The general absence of the nobles denied the Scots army many of their well-armed and trained retainers, which normally comprised their everyday bodyguard and entourage. This presence would have provided an experienced and resolute 'cutting edge' in the battle. However, a commander has to work with what he has, and so, the salient question; would their absence prove crucial? I believe that the English commanders considered it would be. And this was factored into their thinking.

The English army had perhaps 10,000, twice the number of Wallace's Scots, this including heavy cavalry, which force perhaps numbered 1,000. They alone would have been some sight, confidence building or terrifying depending. The English were confident; only a month earlier they had intimidated another Scottish army into surrender. And they had an even lower opinion of this one that faced them now, calling them rogues and thieves. They believed that they only had to bring them to battle to defeat them.

Comparing their own numbers and total superiority in cavalry with the Scots who faced them, there could only be one outcome. Confident is good. There was no way this rabble could beat them, they must have reckoned. Too confident is bad, and the agent of its own correction. The Scots might have looked like a rabble, but they were not. Their confidence too was high. Their resolve even more so. These men were not the servants and retainers of lords there by obligation. They were free men there by choice. This choice was an exercise of will. From this will flowed resolve which their enemy had not appreciated – not yet!

Some of the experienced commanders urged caution in going over the bridge which separated the armies. Indeed, one Scots lord with the English, allegedly Sir Richard Lundie, suggested a flanking movement using cavalry and the ford further along the river. This was rejected. It has always been claimed that Hugh de Cressingham, one of the army's commanders and King Edward's governors in Scotland, was keen to get the fight going. And the most direct route to the Scots was by the bridge. He insisted on using it, perhaps fearing that too much time spent readying his men would allow the Scots to retreat. While this is a reasonable assumption, it still seems strange that the advice to use the ford as well as the bridge was ignored. Perhaps Cressingham did not trust advice from the Scot; fearing that once out of sight some treachery might occur. This was a most natural conclusion, as some evidence suggest that that same Scottish knight was one of Wallace's earliest baronial supporters and possibly even with Wallace when Sheriff Haselrig was killed. This last fact (if such it is) would not have been known to Cresssingham, but either way the instinct not to trust the Scottish noble was a strong and sensible one; best keep any Scots in sight! Anyway, Cressingham concluded, his army was too powerful to be opposed crossing the bridge. There was no need to divide his command.

Like Wallace, Cressingham too was anxious to settle the issue of who ran Scotland. As he would have seen it, there had been too much time wasting and all at the king's expense. The Scots were just over the bridge; get over there and into them before they change their minds, like at Irvine. Had it wished, the Scottish army could probably have retreated fairly easily, at least at the early stage when the English were crossing the bridge and forming up. The mounted English could have pursued them, but given the boggy, hilly and forested terrain, not very effectively. Nothing though would be resolved by this; from the English commander's viewpoint, this was the worst outcome. Well, almost so, barring the unthinkable, a defeat. Cressingham probably thought too that the visible presence of his soldiers crossing over the bridge to form up in front of the Scots would provide the incentive that would prevent the Scots retreating, like a kind of bait. And the crushing victory which would surely follow, would be a perfect end to a frustrating summer. As his troops started across the bridge, at the back of his mind was he composing his victory letter to the king? The Scots let them cross.

Here we enter the minds of the commanders and soldiers. The English commanders probably concluded that the Scots would continue to occupy the high rocky ground and were planning a defensive battle. Having few cavalry and being untried and relatively untrained, a manoeuvring battle on the lower ground below would be beyond them. The cavalry would outflank them. And too, generally lacking in heavier protective armour, they would not be able to match the English men-at-arms in a melee. These are entirely logical conclusions. With the advantage of the high ground they would perhaps be able to resist an attack or two, but they would eventually be broken. The archers would see to that, with the hill now becoming a trap in which they would only come off it dead. Or, if they panicked and ran, the cavalry would ride them down and finish the job until darkness brought these fleeing remnants safety.

Wallace and Moray's options were more limited in terms of their available strategies. Having a smaller and less well equipped force meant they could not afford to engage in a battle of attrition, even a Pyrrhic victory for the Scots would be a strategic victory for the English. Having very little cavalry meant that they could not pursue a broken fleeing army to achieve an eventual victory. Victory would have to be achieved in the battle itself and it would have to be total if Scotland was to be liberated. It would not do much good for the Scots to win the fight and have the defeated army flee but, having sustained relatively low casualties, reform soon after. Looking down as the English formed a defensive perimeter as their army came over the bridge and formed up, it must have been clear that they could not allow their entire army to do this. However, if they attacked too soon, all that would achieve would be to prevent the battle from happening as most of the English would not be able to cross the bridge to join the fight. A useless stalemate. For them waiting, then, the timing was crucial. Wait, wait, still wait…! It must have been a hard wait, seeing the number of the English mount and wondering, second by second, if they were leaving it a bit late.

But then, the moment arrived. Between a third and a half of the enemy had crossed the bridge. The area around the bridge end would have been congested, the soldiers forming up with their backs to the river and no place to move, the ground boggy. The Scots attacked.

This is often imagined as a charge, sometimes it is presented as such. This is false and perhaps only the last few yards, as the opposing front ranks met, would have seen a charge. Indeed, the idea of a wild charge, glorious and visually appealing though it is, does dis-service to the amount of training and discipline required for a large and dense body of spearmen to move across uneven ground and maintain formation. This last point is crucial in the battle that followed.

The extremely long spears that the scots carried made it impossible to sustain a run, and especially a charge, within a packed body of men many hundreds if not 1,000 strong per regiment.

The English would have seen the Scots coming off the hill, perhaps briefly considered whether the manoeuvrings were part of a retreat; with those clearly forming up as a part of a rearguard to allow their comrades a safe escape. But then, as the Scots advanced, they would have realised their intention. These few minutes of uncertainty would prove crucial to the speed of the English deployment and response. At that moment, and in that congested situation where everyone was still forming up, they themselves were not in a position to be able to advance to meet the Scots halfway, But their front line would hurriedly adopt a defensive posture and the archers would have got busy as soon as the Scots got in range, say from 300 yards or so.

The actual deployment of the various Scottish formations that advanced to combat will never be known, but it had to be properly timed, managed and cleverly arranged. But not so clever it compromised the one essential; this was that the Scottish regiments of spearmen meet the enemy line still in formation as a solid mass. It did. This carried the momentum to force the English first line back on itself, denying it space to move or even defend itself, pushing it back onto even muddier ground and, for those English soldiers at the back of the ranks, onto the banks of the river. The first rank of English troops were skewered or crushed by the juggernaut. In seconds this created the physical conditions in front and underfoot for what was to follow. It was an ideal situation for the long Scottish spears. It was now a battle that better suited the skill level and temperament of the Scot. In a way, once the two opposing ranks locked, the rest was consequence.

The situation for many, perhaps even most, of the English soldiers in the middle of this melee would be like a big crowd coming out from a football match; helpless and useless. The river's course had shaped the terrain that the English stood on in such a way that they were surrounded, back and sides, by water. There was no possibility of the troops at the edge of their formation moving wide and flanking the Scots. There was just no land to do this. Those trapped at the rear did not have the option of escaping along the banks due to the same bottleneck. The River Forth here is wide and deep, a decent or desperate swimmer could swim to safety, but given the press of men there would be no opportunity to prepare for such a swim by discarding strapped on armour or chain-mail. Only the lightly armoured would stand a chance, if they could swim at all. And many would not. As the Scots pressed ever forward, more men would be pushed into the water. The sense of frustration and helplessness of those in the middle and rear would be balanced by the desperation of the English front rank, which was denied effective space to fight by the press of Scottish spears in front and a bloody floor of their dead comrades underneath.

What was happening to the English army north of the river was exactly as the experienced English soldiers had feared. Trapped in a bottleneck of land with no escape, crushed and drowned at the back, cavalry and archers rendered useless, the front rank getting killed and forced ever backwards, layer by layer, by the relentless long Scottish spears. In the chaos around the bridge head there was no possibility of reinforcements coming over. In any case, those who could escape by bridge were trying to do so.

The bridge itself was not designed for the weight and chaos that now sat on it, and it partly collapsed separating permanently the English army. Those safe on the south who could only watch in horror as their comrades to the north were slaughtered. There would be no surrender here, for the vast majority it was to the death. This fate must have been apparent from very soon after the battle started and would be confirmed by the collapse of the bridge.

Legend has Wallace having the bridge weakened to achieve this effect. This is doubtful. It would be a simple matter for the English to confirm if such a thing had been done. And too, other than collapsing at the right moment such a weakening would serve no purpose. There is no way in the heat of battle such timing could have been achieved. The breaking of the bridge is also attributed to the English commander. He could hardly have ordered such a thing while his own men were trying to escape, but it is possible that right at the end when he had resolved to flee that this was done to prevent the Scots using it in pursuit.

What a mess it was on the north side. The Scottish cries of triumph mingled with the curses and cries of the defeated English and the fearful whinnying of their horses. The English on the safe side fled for Berwick. The charge (to safety) led by their commander, The Earl of Surrey.

It was at this point, the battle's result having been decided, that the Scottish lords, The Steward and Earl of Lennox with their lesser titled supporters, played their true hand and joined their countrymen. Being mounted they would have ensured that any who escaped the battlefield were killed. Lost and disorganised soldiers become just running men easily rode down; the broken and boggy landscape, dotted with pools (called pows in Scots), lending itself to this task. The nobles also attacked and captured the English baggage train. It is unlikely that any English survived that fight. What started as a battle, ended as a massacre.

It was a great day for the Scots army, for Wallace and Moray their commanders. English losses were very great, perhaps half the army or more. The eventual casualty list not just being confined to the actual fight, but also sustained over the next few days as the foot soldiers made their way south.

It was rare indeed for outnumbered foot soldiers, and mainly as lightly armoured spearmen, to beat mounted armoured knights and men-at-arms. It says much for the quality of their leadership and courage. And it takes away nothing from this achievement to note the exceptional circumstances that made this generally unlikely possibility possible.

The actual location of the battle is probably one of the few places in Scotland where a battle between the Scots and English armies so composed as they were at Stirling Bridge could be fought with the Scots having a chance of success. And it was as near to an ambush as a full scale battle could ever get. The hemmed in and muddy nature of the terrain cancelling out the cavalry advantage, the river at the English backs, an inadequate bridge creating a bottleneck, the Welsh mercenary longbowmen unable to form up and properly see their targets in the melee, the army split into two non-contacting parts, and lastly a gigantic and fatal under-estimating of their foe. This last point itself part of the fated circumstances following on from the capitulation of the Scots nobles at Irvine.

The battle's outcome could be due simply to luck and judgement, good or bad depending on your nationality. But you wonder about other factors. The lack of the king's powerful presence may have, it could be argued, somewhat undermined the unity and purpose he would have brought. But still, the Earl of Surrey was an old and experienced soldier and there was no lack of military experience in the English camp. I believe that the English commanders were distracted and frustrated by the events at Irvine whose protracted negotiations lengthened the campaign (and its costs) and this pressured their judgement. And also, the Irvine surrender introduced into their army Scottish elements, which had to be considered and accommodated, but which they, rightly, did not trust. Finally, Welsh mercenary archers were included in significant numbers for the first time in an English army. Given their stormy relationship to England, their recent conquest, and their separate language, they too did not yet enjoy the full trust of later campaigns in France, and their tactical incorporation into the manual of warfare not yet refined.

I believe that the English strategy was to keep the Scots in sight, both enemies and allies. Trusting that Wallace and Moray's force would not have the skill (or stupidity) to effectively attack. When that actually happened, at first they were not so concerned thinking it would come to nothing. But were then shocked to inaction when it did. This compounded when their Scots 'allies' betrayed them. The capture of the baggage train must have been the final straw.

Surrey seeing his army being crushed, his sustenance for the campaign captured, and not trusting those Scots and Welsh still with him. I think he thought: *Well, this is why I have a horse. Let's save what we can and go.*

Towart Dunbar in gret haist maid thaim boune, as Blind Harry has it.

Fight or flight is a basic animal reflex; only the most able generals are able to hold this in check during a battle when things start to go wrong and keep commanding. This sort of breakdown is fairly common in commanders faced with disaster. And once the general flees, the men follow. And yet the mounted force Surrey fled with and the others abandoned on the south of the river to follow as best they could, was still a significant force and unharmed. It matched in size the victorious Scots army. A resolute commander could have accepted the loss at the bridge, rallied his men, and carried on with the campaign; or, at least, tried. Initially, as a good first move, perhaps trying to win back the captured baggage train. Surrey's mind was broken, the other senior commanders seem to have followed their leader's cue.

Those with horses would make the escape fairly easily, probably with one overnight stop. Those on foot, it depends. It is about 100 miles journey to safety in Berwick and a relatively simple route following the coast from Edinburgh east then southwards. Those soldiers who could keep in a large group would be relatively safe, being big enough to protect themselves. But it would have been a hard 3 or 4 days, with no cavalry to protect their flanks, no baggage and no food. Those who got separated would need lots of luck. Many would not have it, the now nameless who met their death in squalid little encounters where they stood no chance.

It is not only the English commanders at the battle who have received a hard judgement from history. The Scots nobles, and their lesser followers, have the dubious distinction of suffering derision from all sides; and not least their own! Their late joining in the fight being viewed as opportunistic, cowardly even, and more out of greed for the contents of the baggage train. This is a misrepresentation of their position. It is no crime to play a scheming game in difficult times; this too serves its purpose in the long view. It is my belief that it was always their intention to join the fight if things seemed to be going well. The *if* was provisional: Duplicitous, absolutely! Principled; partly. Stupid; no. We must remind ourselves that, prior to the battle, Wallace's army was as yet untried, as was Wallace as a battlefield general. What purpose would it serve the nobles, or Scotland's cause, to embrace the destruction they had avoided at Irvine. The actual result was as much a surprise for them, as for the defeated

English. To my mind, it says something complimentary about their integrity and commitment to their country, that they joined the fight. They need not have, and could have safely sat out the battle and its aftermath, without risking the report that would go to King Edward.

Their full contribution to the actual fight will never be known, but even the noted one of riding down and dispatching the broken formations and fleeing remnants was not insignificant. For it changed the battle from a rout, to a crushing victory or, to phrase it less triumphantly, a massacre. Thus removing the possibility of the fleeing enemy recovering their wits and rallying, or just making good their escape. And also the early capture of the baggage train was crucial, not just for the various sort of supplies and equipment which their own impoverished army would welcome, but also to prevent it being destroyed by its fleeing former guards; no doubt taking with them the most valuable and compromising material, money, private treasures and documents.

The Battle of Stirling Bridge was a relatively small battle as battles go, but it is a great and significant battle in Scottish and British history. Without that victory it is hard to see how Scotland could have resisted being incorporated into England. So many future events that were to lead to the proper re-establishment of our independence were contingent on it; the manoeuvring of Robert the Bruce, for example, could not have happened as they did.

At the time it was the confidence booster that the Scots needed. It proved to themselves God's favour in their cause, and the church would have lost no opportunity to emphasize that point. It proved that with the right tactics and terrain the English could be beaten. It proved to Scottish supporters abroad that the Scots were resolved and able. It is hard to know what it proved to our exiled and erstwhile king, King John of Scotland. What sort of groan did he give on the news?

Scottish losses were relatively light, perhaps a few hundred, and only a bad injury to Moray had potentially serious implications for the cause. But despite the deaths and injuries, there was much to celebrate. All the planning and hardship, the uncertainty of the dark days since the Battle of Dunbar had been put right. The English had got their just desserts. They had now lost all control of the country and had no immediate prospect of winning it back.

There is a gruesome tale associated with the battle's aftermath; the dead English commander and appointed treasurer for conquered Scotland, Cressingham, was flayed and his skin made into a sword-belt which was worn by Wallace. While this is possible and such things not unknown in this bloody age, there is not much precedence for it in the Christianised West. This story has a long pedigree, going back to Wallace's days, but this does not make it true. Nor does the barbarian cruelty of the act sit easily with Scots' attempts to legitimise their mission. It smacks of propaganda, but by whom?

In every age, and our own is just as gullible, enemies are de-humanised by their purported, and exquisite, barbarity. Often too, the subject of such claims, rather than pointlessly deny them, adopt them in defiance as a sort of reverse compliment. Which becomes, in turn, black propaganda. It's not necessarily a bad thing to have your enemy believe that you are capable of anything.

I'm Wallace, and I make belts from my enemy's skin! One's reputation precedes one; and a bad one moves so much quicker.

INTO ENGLAND

**The Battle of Stirling Bridge made Wallace both
the saviour and the leader of his country.**

His authority could not be denied, although he was
careful to emphasize that this was done in the name of his
deposed king. We have no reason to believe that he was
not absolutely sincere in this.

Scotland moved quickly to recognise the new order.
A special committee of nobles and bishops made
Wallace and Andrew Moray the Guardians of Scotland.
This title and the governing role that came, as we have
already mentioned, pre-dated Balliol's kingship and had
legitimacy. Wallace was also knighted and was now Sir
William Wallace, this honour further strengthened his
authority in this age where titles were a necessary part
of political power. It also put him on the same social level
as Moray, a necessary symbol if they were to function as
a Guardianship team of equals. Wallace might still be an
upstart, but he was a titled upstart now. The title won in a
way that our medieval ancestors genuinely respected.

We must bear in mind, though, that catapulted like this
from rebel band captain to leader of his country is a

singular thing to happen to someone and a rare event in history. It was a social journey across class boundaries which has no obvious modern equivalent. Wallace would always be a bit of an outsider in that situation with his putative 'betters', now suddenly 'equals'. Not intending to be a rebel to his society's norms, he must have found this new setting a psychological challenge of the first order. The same, surely, for at least some of his new-found lordly comrades.

The new Guardians' first decisions concerned the army. It was still ready for action, high in confidence and essentially undamaged by the battle and probably significantly reinforced by noble involvement and the recruitment that success encourages. After the celebrations Wallace took the army to Berwick and recaptured it. Moray was not involved in this as his injuries obliged him to stay behind. After Berwick, Wallace's next plan was the invasion of England. No doubt as news of the plans for an invasion of England spread, the army would have received even more recruits eager for revenge and booty. The latter always a great attraction for Scots. By October they were ready.

It was late in the year for marching, but Scots have long been noted for being hardy. And in enduring poor weather and rough conditions. Anyway, by October the English harvest would be in and there would be more to eat and steal; thus lessening supply problems. It would have been a keen army that crossed the border. Keen to teach the

English a lesson. And what a lesson! Plunder and rapine being the subjects taught.

No-one could stop Wallace's Scots army as it rampaged unimpeded through the north of England. The soldiers took a cruel revenge on the English people. Most fled with what they could carry, either to the fortified towns of Newcastle and Carlisle, or southwards. Those that did not escape or were caught by marauding horse troopers would have their fate decided on the moment by fortune. Sympathy is a powerful motive, but so is revenge. And a kindlier captain could see such captives keep their lives, if not their possessions. One thing is sure, the slightest resistance, particularly for men, would have brought instant death.

Anything that could be stolen was stolen, anything that could be burned was burned, any military (or military looking) men would be put to the sword for the slightest of reasons, or none at all. This is an ugly business. It was bad luck to be English that autumn.

King Edward was over the sea in Flanders with his army. Wallace had destroyed the other English army at Stirling, so the northern English were defenceless. If nothing human could stop Wallace, it was time to try the divine. The local saint, Saint Cuthbert, was called upon to intervene. Perhaps in answer he sent colder than normal weather to impede the Scots and make their night camps even more miserable. It was already November. Time to get home before they froze to death. Weighed down with plunder and driving stolen farm stock, they headed for their own hearths. It had been some year.

For Wallace, though, we can be sure that there was no sitting around a fire telling of his successes. There was much to be done if Scotland was to keep her newly won freedom. And Wallace would have to do it alone, for Moray had died while the army was sacking England. Wallace was now the sole Guardian.

The task of Guardian was one that demanded more than the military prowess that Wallace had just displayed. But not for him the chance to ease into the task. In the space of six months he had 'went from being an unknown outsider of no significant status to being in a position of supreme power in his own country. The power and adulation that accompanies it would arguably feel nice for a while. But with the power comes responsibility. And this would be gigantic and relentless and, in a country as factional as Scotland, complicated and full of blame. It was a task that demanded the full array of diplomatic skills and an unusual level of wisdom in young man of action. As a warrior chief, we can easily imagine Wallace as resolute and plain talking, but charm and subtlety were required too.Wallace did not need told that Scotland was not a country that could be bullied.

The immediate task; finance, train and maintain the army. Keep friends with other countries who could help, especially France and our neighbours in the Low Countries and the Baltic. He would have to encourage the nobles in Scotland to declare their commitment and join the fight. And if they did, keep them from bickering among themselves. For it never took much to get the Scots nobles to draw daggers on each other. In this age of carrying weapons, this phrase also packs a literal meaning.

Bringing the Scots together to face a common foe was the hardest task for Scotland had so many fault lines: tribal, baronial, linguistic, even ethnic. From Wallace's viewpoint, the crucial one was the attitude to the deposed king and his wider family and supporters in Scotland. This was a fault line that ran all the way back to the tragic death of the Maid of Norway. Realistically, it was a problem that could not be fixed, especially while the king was alive and in exile.

Wallace had the church and the common people behind him. But some of the most powerful families, the Bruces for example, were in two minds. Firstly, there was the issue of Wallace personally, this man from a lesser social level running the country. The outsider who suddenly achieves power and influence is always the subject of suspicion and jealousy. And, more importantly, they did not want to side with Wallace, only to get beaten again by King Edward the next year, when he returned in person. Which they knew he would. And this time not at all kindly disposed to yet some other deal with the Scots nobles.

However, whatever their misgivings, most of them kept quiet. 'Ca canny', and see what the next year brings when it comes. The large and successful army Wallace still commanded was an authority they could respect. Wallace was in charge.

IN POWER

King Edward's absent presence was included in all the celebrations back in Scotland. That most unwelcome of visitors, a revenant. He would be back.

Wallace knew that the present liberation of Scotland would be a temporary thing. The English king would have to'be defeated more decisively than at Stirling Bridge. He would have regarded the defeat merely as a setback. As a military man he would have understood the details of the defeat seeing it correctly as a combination of bad luck, treachery and poor generalship. All in all, an exception that would not be repeated. Especially, if he was there in person.

Scotland's only hope lay in being unified against this threat. Stand together or fall together, being the presented rationale. Looking back, it may seem that achieving this unity should not present too much of a problem. After all, the English were foreign invaders. King Edward had invaded because, bottom line, he wanted to and he could. The sense of injustice surrounding this we know was great. And few Scots were in favour of their country being incorporated into greater England. However, although our ancestors would have recognised these facts, they did not live in an age of simple choices.

We look back on the bare bones of history and miss the web of factors and forces that animated our ancestors' lives. Like us, they too lived by ideas which shaped their understanding of who they were. Medieval ideas about fate, justice, honour, while not entirely different to ours today, are not the same either. For these were ideas whose full expression had an absolute quality, how you thought and acted really could get you killed. And being killed or otherwise dying was a fate that was always close by. It makes culture somewhat fatalistic, and being so makes the ideas attendant on fate, like justice, honour, loyalty, more strongly held. Societies under stress often tend to embrace the full fatalistic panoply of such concepts. This can be a source of their resilience, but so easily segues to fanaticism.

Medieval life was not, of course, lived in the head. It was immensely practical, and so the duties and obligations, likes and dislikes, that connect us with our family and friends, also have to be added to the mix. They were just as tied up in politics and family and self-interest as we are. Just as irrational and stubborn. With two massively important distinctions; the presence of God and the need for his approval. And, secondly, medieval judgements being famously peremptory, if you made a bad choice, the consequences could be lethal very quickly.

Unlike the vast majority of Scots who had no connection whatsoever with England, some nobles had estates and relatives in England, and perhaps considered themselves as members of a ruling elite rather than Scots or English as such. Some, perhaps, who had French as their first or preferred language would have looked to the Francophile world for their cultural identity. Many of these may not have necessarily seen this as a national issue, nor thought their national or cultural identity was relevant in this dispute. Seeing it as a dynastic thing, at least at first. They, as many in our own time whose families straddle two cultures, would have been distressed to have to choose an allegiance.

Many Scottish nobles were no doubt confused, not only about where their best interests lay, but what they actually felt. Alas, war does not allow fence sitting. Hopefully, though, this reflection on the various invisible factors informing our ancestors' opinions and actions will help us understand the disparity of their responses. Something that all the main protagonists in this story had to deal with.

Aware of the pressures that could force the Scots nobles to oppose him, King Edward had taken hostages to England, mainly sons. These would be treated well, of course, but what if the king was crossed? These hostages were not symbolic; the execution of the Welsh princely hostages in King John's reign would be well known. And even discounting, if you could, the thought of this severest of retributions, having your children possibly forever lost in the hostage situation would be an emotional nightmare to contend with.

And then, the big question, who would, or should be, the King of Scots if Wallace was successful?

Not everyone wanted King John back, especially the Bruce family who had long harboured legitimate hopes of the throne. A lot of the humming and hawing connected to this point. Should the Bruces and their supporters fight for Scotland and to hell with the consequences? If so, should they take a leading role, as befitted their status, or stay in the background? And what exactly would they be fighting for; the return of King John. Why would they want that, they must have thought. If for them, the only issue was winning Scotland's crown, would it not be better to stay in favour with the English in the hope that some deal could be reached with Edward or the next king? There was no simple answer to these questions for the Bruces, as is still the case, even with hindsight!

All Scotland's noble families were roped into this Bruce/ Balliol question whether they liked it or not. Of course, they wanted to do their best for their country, but perhaps not so strongly, or at all, if old rivals would end up better off. Some also would have been aware, in a direct way that would naturally be beyond the experience of most Scots, of the great disparity in wealth and size between Scotland and England, and they must have argued this point. (Although, ironically perhaps, this difference was much greater, ten times or more, say, than they could ever have considered.) Scotland, the brave mouse facing the English cat. The outcome, obvious and inevitable.

The one certainty in the nobles' considerations was that King Edward would be back, his army would be more formidable than that defeated at Stirling Bridge and he would not be pleased. Freedom of conscience for Scotland's noble families was to be bought at a high price; the loss of life, estate, fortune and the ignominy of failing to satisfy their lordly duty to their dependents *and* their ancestors. The privileges of rank are not always enjoyable.

Many have found it easy to present the nobles as a cowardly and duplicitous bunch, but this is a viewpoint informed by modern political sensibilities and is ignorant of actual context. No rational person embraces self-destruction. And the nobles cannot be fairly criticised for not choosing to embrace a simple idea of integrity and nationality that is of our manufacture, when we ourselves would act as they did. That they may have been duplicitous says nothing of note, as we all are when our interests are threatened. And cowardly? Scotland's history provides solid evidence again and again that this class did not lack bravery.

During this period while the nobles may have been soul searching, Wallace must have been extremely busy. One thing we can be sure of is that he could have had no experience of doing such a job. And although this age predates mass literacy, the administration of government and trade generated a surprising amount of paperwork and documents. Clerks and managing clerics would carry on the day to day aspect and he could rely on the experience of the church and chancellery managers, but the final responsibility would fall on the Guardian. He had political authority, but could he bring energy and wisdom to the job?

We just have one precious communication from this period, an official letter to the cities of Lubeck and Hamburg, informing them that Scotland was open for trade again as an independent realm. Of course, this letter was not personally written by Wallace, but it does have his seal as Guardian.

This, as administration always is, would be an endless and thankless task. But absolutely vital. A band of brigands, or a clan raid doesn't need paperwork. But a country does. Trade and justice and finances all need managing, decisions have to be promulgated, a proper army can only be maintained by effective mustering, training, equipping and feeding, all of which has to be organised and accounted. And above all, Scotland had to find friends (which would be easy!), but especially friends with money and influence (which is never easy!) For here the potential friends are compromised in like fashion to Scotland's nobles. This diplomatic effort is almost invisible to us now, but would have been especially vigorous in the Wallace's 'breaking in period' to Guardianship. It required much subtlety of presentation to ensure that Wallace appeared as a credible and legitimate figure. Of course, King Edward was well aware that such activity was taking place and would ensure his own diplomats and agents were ensuring the Scots' effort was cancelled out.

King Edward will be back. And this has to be planned for. Paperwork, talking, meetings. Wallace we are sure was a man of plain words, but Scotland's nobles were also plain talking men too. Subtlety usually carries further. The last thing Wallace needed was to make more enemies and in persuading all to join the cause he needed to know when to push a point and when to defer. He would have to be able to deal with the nobles on an equal footing, without offending the codes of behaviour that governed that society. This is common sense, but it is one thing to know this and another to act it. And here, perhaps, this argues for a subtlety on Wallace's part to balance out the steel. The veiled threat has a place, but is still a threat and has to be used judiciously. Did some of those who needed a 'bit of a push' to commit, find themselves persuaded by the thought that their heads might end up looking out of a basket if they went against Wallace? We will never know how much Wallace's style depended on this.

When referring to Wallace and his dealings with the nobles and how crucial they were, we must not forget that Wallace's power base was the army manned by the commons. And these too would have to be fully considered in his decisions. This made Wallace different; kings or barons needed to give thought to the welfare of their followers, but not their opinions. However, the army Wallace now led was brought together by his fame and leadership, but held together thereafter by his personal qualities. This army of the commons needed to feel that he was with them, not above them. His nobility was in his spirit and example, not his blood-line. They needed to feel that he wasn't using them to climb the social ladder. He would need the 'common touch'; only the greatest of captains in the history of warfare have been able to combine the roles of leader and comrade. How was Wallace able to do this, as we know this was not a prerogative of his birth, nor had his training so far as we know prepared him? Here we are speculating on the mystery of personality. And nothing we write or think takes us nearer to adequately defining, far less understanding, what that quality is. The cliché 'cometh the hour, cometh the man' seems especially apt. If Scotland was to survive in any meaningful way then it needed a Wallace just at the point he arrived.

- If he didn't know it beforehand, it was as Guardian that Wallace would have learned that the forces that made Scotland strong; the forces that brought him an army to face the English, the independence of spirit, the hardiness, the loyalty to family, the willingness to fight and that wild streak that ran through Scottish character like marbling, were the same forces that could and would blow it apart. The frustration sometimes must have been overwhelming. The appetite for civil war was surely lessened at this time, but the danger was still there. And it required diplomatic skills of great subtlety and sometimes necessary ruthlessness to keep the Scots united. Wallace seems to have achieved this following Stirling Bridge. Hopes were high, perhaps some deal with King Edward could be achieved after all, perhaps (and I think this was the stronger hope) the king would die on campaign in France as he was not a young man, now nearly 60. In this early optimism, it might have felt like endgame. And this helped keep everyone united. They were not to know that this war would run for generations.

During this period Wallace must have been practically living in his saddle. We can picture him with his hird ⁻ riding over a landscape of snow. All happed up in enormous riding capes. Breath hanging in the air. Swords always handy. The strain, the tiredness, the uncertainty would take a toll. We can see him in a great hall, back to a roaring fire, wondering if the Pope, a friend to the Scots at this time, could be persuaded to do more for the cause.

Something of Wallace's greatness is proven during this period. For with this sudden power, is sudden temptation. It would have tempted many beyond their powers of resistance. Family and friends can always be helped and, of course, lining your own pocket is very easy to justify. He had done his duty by his country, it could be argued, now was time for peace with England. It was a real possibility, thought if not suggested, that he could negotiate a surrender with King Edward and do well for himself and his kin out of it. The English king was magnanimous, a king's prerogative, when it suited him. One thing is sure, if Wallace had abused his power in this way we would have heard of it. Wallace served just one cause; his country and her rightful king. He was careful to say so.

More than anyone Wallace pulled the country back from the brink of an extinction of gradual incorporation into England, and then united it in the following year against the inevitable return of King Edward. But we must remember the others too who stood with him. Andrew Moray, tragically killed before he could establish the reputation he probably deserved. The hard, angry men of the original resistance gangs that did the cruel dagger work that got the ball rolling. And the others who joined Wallace and Moray at Stirling, and then after into England, proving at spearpoint that they cared for their country. The men and women who could not fight, but gave succour to rebels when to do so was to risk ruination. And the same for the nobles who cast aside the complications of their position and joined the cause. And finally, the church, providing that crucial practical support and the necessary justification of conscience so important in our ancestors' religious beliefs.

What all these people were risking became evident by the summer of 1298. King Edward had come back from Flanders and was personally set on punishing the Scots. The deal he had made to their faces after deposing King John, the promise they had signed in the Ragman's Rolls, their word to him, had been broken. He was angry.

THE BATTLE OF FALKIRK

**When King Edward came home from France
he immediately set about planning a fresh
invasion of Scotland.**

Being a revenge mission the king had little bother
recruiting for the campaign. The English knights in
particular wanting to make amends and re-establish
their reputation. The king's army, perhaps 20,000 strong,
contained a significant number of archers and knights,
two components of which the Scots were always short.
It was arranged for the army to be supplied by ships
dropping off provisions along the coast. A neat solution to
the problem of extended supply lines and the likelihood
of finding nothing to eat once over the border. By July
1298 the English were at Roxburgh and ready to begin
the punishment.

The English marched through the Borders and Lothian
destroying everything in their path. They found no people,
all had fled with their beasts. Neither was the Scots army
anywhere to be seen.

Wallace was being cautious. The Lothians especially,
being open country, did not allow a surprise attack and

was ideal country for cavalry and archers. This was not the place to oppose them. Nor, while fresh and optimistic at the start of their campaign, the time. Let them come on.

We cannot know Wallace's intentions. However, it seems obvious that his priority was to keep the army intact and avoid battle, unless favourable circumstances presented themselves. The English were wanting a pitched battle, a good general does not oblige his enemies. The strategy then would have to be flexible. Let the English advance through an evacuated land, extending their supply lines and moving into more rugged and hilly country. As they moved northwards they increasingly moved into a countryside built by nature for defence and ambush. And, as the journey took its toll in tiredness and frustration, wait for an opportunity. Even if none occurred, that would still not be a failure for the Scots. The English army was an army of campaign, not of occupation, and they were in Scotland to force the Scots to battle. If none occurred within the summer season and service conditions of the soldiers, then they would have to go home. Both armies would be frustrated at this outcome, but without doubt the Scots could regard such an apparently neutral outcome as a victory and the English as a defeat. At enormous cost, and to his prestige too, King Edward would have achieved nothing. The Scots would still have an army and would still be in charge.

The absence of the enemy caused frustration in the king's army. Having no enemy outlet it would turn on itself. To make matters worse, the ships were proving unreliable in supplying the army. The soldiers, still unable to live off the land, were becoming increasingly hungry. By the time the army was at Kirkliston, within straight-line sight of Edinburgh Castle, it was in a bad way; hungry and demoralised. The Welsh archers, so recently enemies (and still so in their hearts, as the English well knew) had fallen out with the English soldiers and some fights had broken out between them. Supplies, discipline and good leadership make an army function as it should. With the supplies problematic, and the discipline becoming fragile, there was a possibility of the army disintegrating. The king was forced to consider his options, one of which was retreat to Edinburgh and begin a withdrawal from Scotland. Wallace's strategy was working, Without having to fight, he was sending the English home defeated.

The Scots could and should regard such an outcome as a victory, but would they. Wallace had a warrior's heart, his army were obviously similarly constituted. The English would go home complaining about the cowardly Scots that would not face them. They would further argue, based on this, that their loss at Stirling Bridge was a one-off; they had given the Scots a chance to repeat it, and they would not. Such a claim, which the Scots knew would be made, would offend their sense of themselves. And too, with no decisive outcome achieved, there was a sense of postponement. The Scots had to win back their independence and their reputation, the English had to be made to feel pain, not just frustration. And this needed a victory.

Being as flat as Scotland ever gets, the terrain around the king's camp near Edinburgh was good horse country, open vistas suited the longbow-men, an open attack was still out of the question. But a night attack on the English camp? This would cancel out English advantages. This could be a perfect souvenir to take home to England.

A night attack on the English camp is easy enough to claim as a plan and, as already noted, seems sensible. But this claim nicely illustrates the problems for the historian. When we consider the formidable obstacles to the success of such a plan we must wonder how likely this claim is to be true. And, if it is, even more fascinating how this was to be achieved.

The Scots would have had good intelligence as to the disposition of the camp, but this would probably not come as a comfort, given that the king's presence should have ensured the highest standards of military preparedness, especially for something like a night attack. And the short nights in high summer seem to limit the possibility of moving a large body of foot soldiers into position secretly before the attack and extracting them before dawn turned the battle into a day battle. We must suppose, then, that what Wallace planned was a mounted raid using local knowledge of the terrain to best advantage. The twenty miles or so between the two armies was do-able for well-mounted men in less than three hours; rest the horses, then attack. The numbers would have to be sufficient to overwhelm the camp defence and cause damage, but clearly could not be so large as to prevent efficient movement at night. Probably we are talking about many hundreds of mounted men. But while this could cause mayhem, it would still lack the weight to do real damage. They would have to flee before the much larger English army was aroused. Ten minutes sword work could be bigged-up later as a significant victory, the hurt to King Edward's pride would not need exaggerated. Unless it absolutely failed, this was a good idea.

But it was betrayed. Two Scottish Earls, of Dunbar and of Angus, who sided with Edward, apparently had a spy who reported the plan and the location of the Scots. Whether due to a spy or not, when King Edward found out where the Scots were, he took his chance to sort out his so far failed campaign. If he could turn the tables on the Scots, make a surprise march to their camp and force them to battle, then all would end well. With great haste he set off for the Scots' camp at Falkirk.

His night raid plan foiled and the English nearby, Wallace's options were dramatically reduced. It is one thing to avoid battle as a strategy, this is acceptable. But to run away from the direct offer, even if logical, is not. This would be presented as cowardice; worse than a defeat. Further, the option of escaping was relatively simple for Wallace's mounted men. However, the spearmen, slower on foot and encumbered with their arms, could have found themselves isolated, outmanoeuvred and eventually surrounded by the king's large number of mounted men. No, Wallace's army had to stay together. The arguments of the hot-heads, who had all along wanted a go at the

English, could not be resisted now. They were not afraid, they had done the impossible at Stirling, why not now too! Besides, they no doubt argued, if they did not deal the English a heavy blow now, they would just come back again next year. A victory against an army with the king's presence was the greatest prize. And temptation! Escape, with competent generalship, would have been possible. But was psychologically a weak choice. Here and now, it had to be decided who was in charge of Scotland.

Is there a sense of resignation about Wallace's supposed words to his army: *I have led you to the ring. Dance if you can!* Perhaps in this there is a grim humour intended that is lost to us now. It was the 22nd July, 1298.

It was not an ideal situation for the smaller Scots army, of perhaps no more than four or five thousand, but they were well-trained, well-motivated and Wallace was their leader. Four schiltroms or regiments of spearmen formed up. The men put on their helmets and said their prayers. Let the English come on.

The battle started when the English heavy cavalry of armoured knights charged the schiltroms. The sound and sight of seeing, say, 500 armoured knights bearing down on you need not be exaggerated and an untrained or undisciplined body of men could not resist fleeing. This is what the English knights expected. The longer Scots spears met the English lances. In a second the thunder of the galloping horses became the crash of metal on metal, the whine of crippled horses, the cries and shouts of men. The long Scots spears would vibrate with the impact, some would crack or splinter having speared an Englishman. Scots would be lanced clean through, or sent flying. Knights would have been thrown from their horses. Horses would collapse mortally wounded sending groups of spearmen tumbling like skittles. The cavalry would have made a big dent which would have rippled through the Scots' formation, but it held and the soldiers stood and fought it out toe to toe. And then, after a struggle, drove the knights away. Those that could. Those left behind, the unhorsed and wounded, would be battered and hacked to death. Their helmets torn off for a killing neck cut, or a dagger through the eye socket. Round one to the Scots! The English cavalry charge although repulsed did have one benefit, perhaps even unintended. It had panicked the smaller Scots cavalry contingent and most fled the field. This element of the army was made up mainly of the nobles and their men. They were not seen again that day.

While the retreated English cavalry recovered and reformed itself, the king instructed his archers, of which he had many thousands, to shoot down the schiltroms. The large, densely packed schiltroms were the easiest of targets, and could be engaged at long (and safe, for the archers) range. Most arrows finding a target, and these being mainly unarmoured men, was an injury or death. It is at this point that the Scots cavalry should have charged into the archers, had they been there. But with them gone, there was no hindrance to thousands upon thousands of arrows pouring out of the sky like rain: 50,000 arrows, perhaps double that, in five minutes. In the chaos of this killing storm, hardly less in effect than machine guns, it would be impossible to coordinate an attack against the archers. Those that could flee, did. And when the deadly stream finally stopped, the reformed knights, supported by men at arms, charged back into the thinned out ranks for the finishing.

For those Scots left standing there was only one fate now. The only option; sell your life dear. The only Scots we know by name were nobles who died at this point. They had not fled on horseback, but stayed behind with the foot soldiers. The other nameless ones bear our names today.

Towards the end, Wallace was persuaded or perhaps dragged from the field and fled to safety with his bodyguard and closest companions. No matter how he felt about it, he could not be allowed to die at Falkirk. He was still his country's leader and was still needed. Others fled as best they could. The boggy, forested and broken nature of the terrain offering some advantage to the escapers if they could make some initial distance between themselves and their pursuers. Those with horses obviously stood the best chance. Wallace himself was hotly pursued for some time by a large force of cavalry. Even here he could strike back. We are told that Sir Brian le Jay and some other knights in the lead of the following group were led into a bog by the Scots and while floundering about were killed. Wallace personally killing le Jay.

But despite these paybacks, there was no denying that the English had won a tremendous victory. The English victory was not Pyrrhic, the Scots defeat not a fighting retreat, nor even a rout with the fleeing army broken but intact. This was a crushing blow.

The exact size of this will never be known. Then, as we easily see in our own time, everything written about a battle serves a propaganda purpose. All the Scots casualties would be deaths. But how many? Those who fled early, and especially the nobles and their mounted men, would have kept their lives. Perhaps some schiltroms, fortunately placed, may have been able to conduct a sort of fighting retreat to the higher ground and woods behind them and then relative safety. While unluckier schiltroms, bearing the brunt of the English assaults, unwittingly provided this opportunity. This seems likely, and the middle placed schiltroms made an escape while the soldiers on the flanks were fighting. Thinking this through, and accepting contemporary accounts of the battle as basically accurate, it seems likely that at least a third and possibly even two thirds of the army were killed, thus between two and five thousand men. Wallace's power base was gone.

English casualties, must have been lighter, perhaps even very light. It all depends on the timing of the various components of the battle. Some of the young bloods, keen to make a name, perhaps closed with the Scots before they need have and paid for this with their lives. Reports of rough parity in battle casualties are, I believe, a sop to

Scottish sensibilities hurt by the defeat. Or an English need to make themselves the victors in a hard hand to hand slog.

Pleased though King Edward was, it was still obvious that the campaign had failed to meet its main objective of reconquering Scotland. English authority had not been restored, The Scots nobles had mostly not submitted to him, the countryside was still full of Scots rebels and, perhaps most grating of all, Wallace was still at large. The king's army was still starving, when they set off for home.

King Edward was to discover, as Wallace had done the year before, that winning a battle does not always win a war, far less solve a problem.

AFTER FALKIRK

**The days following Falkirk were very dark ones.
Would the country go to King Edward now?**

———◆———

Winning is easy to live with. Until Falkirk, Wallace had
been a hero. Now what was he? His army had been
defeated, as all armies are eventually, but was he more
than just another defeated general? His enemies would
claim so; he was the imposter unmasked, the jumped-
up commoner slapped back down to his rightful place,
the coward who had fled before the king's army as the
king had predicted he would. And the half-truth in these
thoughts must have stung. Pride humbled.

That they were outnumbered, were perhaps the victims
of treachery, had matched the enemy blow for blow until
undone by the irresistible power of the longbow, and
that many had made an escape would provide some
comfort, but not much. Wallace must have been thrown
into despair, flashed with anger, frustration, regret. This
moment was Wallace's true test. This moment marks the
difference between a warrior and a general. The warrior
can lament, the general must reorganise. There were
practical things to be done.

King Edward would have felt that the rightful order of things had been restored and must have expected in the days following his victory that the Scots would have come to him as supplicants. But they didn't. They had been beaten in a battle, but not defeated for their spirit had not been crushed. The Scottish resistance had not collapsed and Scots still ran the country. But for how long? At this point, in the days and early weeks following the Battle of Falkirk, was a test of nerves for everyone. At this point, more than ever perhaps, Wallace's presence was needed to help the Scots stand firm.

Some Scots lords had, of course, already came into the 'king's peace' as surrendering to him was termed. And after news of Falkirk the others must have thought of it. That it didn't happen is proof, at its simplest, that the defeat was not a catastrophic one, nor the tipping point. Although it could have been. Wallace, in concert with other patriots (as they would have seen themselves), was able to persuade by argument, and by the fact of still being there, to hold fast.

The English king was running out of time, everyone knew this. By the terms of service, much of his army would have to go home. Any Scots that may have been swaying towards the king's peace would be aware of their own precarious situation when he did go. King Edward could, of course, persuade or bully some of his army into staying longer if he wished, but this would cost him. And too, compromise the goodwill that even the strongest of kings has to keep with his subjects.

Flexible, when it suited him, Edward fell back on that kingly prerogative; diplomacy. A kindly gesture from a position of power is the hallmark of a great and wise king. As Shakespeare was to observe later: the gentlest gamer is the soonest winner when kingdoms are at stake.

If the king could get Wallace to surrender with his men and their supporters in the church, then surely the Scottish resistance would collapse. Only a few wild men, and Balliol diehards would be left outside the peace process. These would be irrelevant and would be hunted down in time. Wallace was offered 'The King's Peace' through some now unknowable channel. For the king's forgiveness, all Wallace would have to do was recognise King Edward as his sovereign and solemnly promise never to rebel again. This was an honourable and generous offer, in the manner of the day. The argument would run; *You've done your duty, but now it's time to be sensible.* Wallace could have surrendered, found pardons for his men, saved face and done well for himself, for no doubt a sweetener would have been added to the deal. In Edward's mind this was an everybody wins situation. The king's reputation massively enhanced by defeating the rebels, but bringing them to his peace by his magnanimity. King Edward, the rebel tamer. Was Wallace tempted?

I think not. And I believe that something essential about his character was revealed by rejecting the king's advance. Obviously, Wallace was true to his cause; the old king's return, Scotland's cause. But this stand reveals a man that was above all true to himself. This certain self-compass, the necessary guide of all principle. While possibly true, this view of Wallace as an essentially moral man is absent from his historiography.

When King Edward heard of the rejection he must have realised that he was dealing with a different type of man from the usual crafty and self-aggrandising types he often encountered. Principled, but dangerously so; for Wallace's response revealed him not as just an honest rarity or even a fanatic, but a radical who thought himself the equal of a king. And while the king might have had a certain regard, respect even for Wallace's integrity, he would have hated what he represented.

Commoners, like Wallace, could not turn down an offer from a king, especially one like King Edward. The offer was actually a polite command. Wallace well knew this. Knew the size of the insult, knew that knowledge of this would spread far afield to the king's embarrassment and knew that there could now only be one ending for himself should Edward prevail. Death as a general in the middle ages was always a strongly possible outcome, with Wallace's insult to the king that outcome shifted much nearer to the certainty. Wallace could not be bought, the king would have to have him killed. Wallace became a prize for a certain type of man, although this was in the future for Wallace still had power and security. Although less of both.

After Falkirk, Wallace still had the support of the common people, his army and the church. Some of the nobility, perhaps many, clearly still supported him. But for others, as we have seen, the right route was not so obvious. Wallace's momentum was gone after Falkirk, it was time for a change. Wallace decided, or was persuaded, that Scotland's cause would best be served by him taking some other role and leaving the leadership of the country to the nobles. In September he resigned as Guardian. New ones were appointed, they included Robert the Bruce, the current Earl of Carrick and our future king, and John III Comyn, Lord of Badenoch, King John Balliol's nephew. Bishop Lamberton was also made Guardian, perhaps as peacekeeper to these traditionally hostile rival families. Although his position as Bishop of Saint Andrews and his diplomatic contacts and experience argued for themselves for his presence. They continued the fight against King Edward.

Had Wallace failed then? Many have argued that he had, pointing to the defeat and subsequent resignation as Guardian. It depends, I suppose, on your standard of success. By the highest standard, probably his own, he had; for he failed to prevent an invasion, defeat the invaders, deliver Scotland's freedom and secure the return of King John. Measured against more realistic standards, even including the defeat, Wallace had not failed. England was a much more populous and wealthy country than Scotland. It was just too big and too united under a strong monarch for Scotland to win its freedom back with a good summer's fighting. Even had the Scots won Falkirk, they would have found themselves in much the same position as their defeat brought.

There was no possibility of Scotland ever fielding an army that could match the English in numbers, resources or equipment. Success for the Scots in this war would, then, depend on endurance. Luck, careful preparation and training, good generalship; these could win them battles, but in the end the vastly greater strength of England must prevail. There were no technological solutions to bridge the gap in power between them. They would have to keep faith with their cause, keep united, hang in and roll with the punches, never give up. Never give up. In this way they could frustrate English ambitions, wear the English down with casualties, empty their coffers, and by so doing ferment dissent at home. Force the English king to choose between his continental possessions and his Scottish ambitions. The hope that this would prevail: *Let them have their ragged kingdom, then! We've got bigger fish to fry in France and Flanders.* Of course, any who knew King Edward would know that this most emphatically would not be his take on Scotland, but who knows how subsequent kings would consider the Scottish problem.

It is in nurturing this spirit, and the practical measures he took to keep the struggle alive at its weakest point, that we have to judge Wallace's success. Scotland did not fall to pieces and into King Edward's lap. Even the fickle nobles did not rush to make peace. Who could have done better? The question is rhetorical.

Three months after Falkirk, King Edward left Scotland. Some castles and towns had been recaptured from the Scots, but apart from this he had gained no significant benefit from his invasion and victory. And all at great cost.

It was almost as if the battle had not happened. Scotland was still free.

WALLACE ABROAD

**Although a Scot, Wallace would also have
regarded himself as a European.**

For nearly a year after the Battle of Falkirk we have no
knowledge of Wallace. Although not in the Guardian's hot
seat any more, he was not a discredited figure and still
had support, and so must have been busy in the Scots'
cause. But doing what? His situation would not allow for
him retiring to a quiet life in his family or a monastery,
even could you imagine such a life for Wallace.

Pressure from Scotland and the French was mounting
at the Pope's court in Rome to oblige King Edward to
release King John. This process was a slipping and sliding
game of promises, half promises, subtle understanding,
implied arrangements, misrepresentations and outright
deceptions played by allies, would-be allies, enemies, and
enemies of enemies. Gaining the Pope's favour was not
a question of demonstrating the righteousness of your
cause. The Pope's role by this time was far removed from
allowing him the indulgence of choosing to follow his
conscience on an issue like the Scots problem. It seems
that the Pope Boniface genuinely was sympathetic to
Scotland, but his judgement on the issue depended on

considering the impact or desirability of such a judgement on the interests of bigger players than Scotland. And Boniface was the very epitome of a scheming, politicised pope, not always respected by his contemporaries (Dante's *Divine Comedy*, for example, has other popes domiciled in hell expecting his arrival, *while* Boniface was actually still alive!) nor kindly regarded by history. Still, he was a friend of Scotland and, at this part of our story, there seemed a chance that some deal could be done that would allow King John to be released from captivity. Whatever the nature of this deal, it would depend upon Scottish unity, as clearly any Scots writing to the Holy Father complaining about such a deal would entirely undermine the whole process, as would news of significant divisions between the Scots themselves. Wallace must have been one of the figures behind the unity of purpose that the Scots demonstrated during the post-Falkirk period.

Some have felt that Wallace would have set himself to punish those responsible for the desertion of the Scots cavalry at Falkirk, as the movie *Braveheart* portrays. However, it is not clear at all what happened at Falkirk. It is possible to describe some Scots nobles as treacherous, if one so wishes to characterise their behaviour thus, but cowardly is generally not a fair description of this class. It seems more likely that the much smaller in number, less well trained and individually much less powerful (man for man and horse for horse) Scottish cavalry were simply swept from the field by the size and strength of the English knights. And while not wishing to deride our

Scottish breeds, which were bred more for robustness, they were not comparable creatures in size, nutrition and training to their equine opponents that day, the English War Horse. We must remember too, that the Scots cavalry (and I include the horse's point of view here, as these have the same rational powers of self-preservation as we do) had not planned or expected to meet their English counterparts, at least, not so suddenly. In a head to head confrontation, such as occurred, no other outcome was possible than the one that happened. Those who could, having fled for their lives (with panicked mounts that were bolting for the same reason) found later their horses blown and themselves scattered and unorganised, and unable or unwilling to return to the fray. Some would have. And perhaps some played some small rearguard role in the escape of the Scots infantry. We have to accept that the lack of recriminations probably indicates that none were required. The nobles' apparent treachery a later fiction to justify Wallace's defeat; the mythic hero's story always has to have betrayals.

Any other disappointments that Wallace may have held regarding the nobles' contribution would have to be laid aside. Blame and punishment would immediately lead to civil war. He knew that it was necessary to stay friendly with the nobles for both political and military reasons. Sure, Wallace could bring an army into the field, but without reliable cavalry it would get shot down by archers, just like at Falkirk. It was the nobles who controlled the cavalry. It was the nobles who controlled, in their retinues, the only year-round military forces

(Wallace's army being, of necessity, seasonal), it was the nobles who held resources, it was the nobles who held power. It was them that ultimately controlled Scotland's destiny. And, to a lesser extent, King John's. Even though they were not always reliable, things simply could not be done without them. This can be hard for us now to understand, for the reality of their social presence is an alien thing to modern sensibilities. And too often, in our failing to appreciate something, we are often led to dismiss it.

The Vatican arranged the release of King John from (comfortable) captivity in the summer of 1299. He returned to France and lived under the Pope's 'protection'. He was, of course, under the conditions of his release, prevented from returning to Scotland. As an added guarantee of his compliance with this ordinance, his son, Edward, remained behind in England as a 'guest' of the English king.

Scotland was still free, some castles excepted, but the situation with the Guardians was tense and uncertain. In fact, two of the Guardians, Bruce and Comyn, both representatives of the former contenders for the throne and, as such, potential contenders themselves, had been brawling at a meeting in Peebles. Perhaps this, as it was a spy's report, may have been an exaggeration. However, as later events were to prove, there can be no question that this happening demonstrated their essential attitude to each other. We do not know why they fought, but whatever the ostensible reason, the underlying one is the unresolvable family rivalry: Can Bruce support the Balliol faction, can the Balliols trust Bruce?

It was a delicate time and Scotland needed powerful friends. These were to be found in continental Europe. Someone would have to go there and see them. Wallace was a natural choice for this mission. Having the prestige of a warrior general, but also, by virtue of not being a senior churchman or noble, being a little bit of a curiosity. This distinction brings some advantage. Wallace was not just another noble supplicant to the European great houses, begging support for a cause. These were ten a penny in this age, he was different and people would be interested to meet him as a result. So, just around the time of King John's release, Wallace left for a European mission as instructed by the Guardians and with the blessing of the church. The nature of the mission, and the nature of travel then, meant that he would be gone for some time, at least a year. We can be fairly sure that the thought of this lengthy trip must have pleased some people in Scotland: *Take your time, William!*

When considered, this mission reveals some things about Wallace. Firstly, his deportment, manners and presence were considered by his peers as equal to the task of this important mission. Secondly, his integrity was not in doubt. Thirdly, his intelligence and education must have been sufficient for the task, and surely above the norm for this age. It is inconceivable, for example, that Wallace was there as a dummy exhibit, while others spoke. And that documents were being written and presented that he could not read. This argues for strong Latin in all its areas and, at least, competent French. Wallace needed subtlety to do this mission well. And perseverance. The subtlety was not just in understanding the complex politics and knowing what to say, but also to understand himself as a symbol of something more than himself. Knowing how people would look on him and then understanding how to play that to best advantage.

In a way, Wallace was a diplomat bringing almost nothing to the table. Some, many perhaps, would be charmed and impressed and deeply moved by Scotland's plight, but who really cared enough to do something? He would find out. And he would need that subtlety of thought to accept and disguise disappointments, and his famous warrior perseverance, somewhat reconfigured to a different sphere, to stay positive with any setbacks.

This mission also revels something about Falkirk and Wallace's conduct there. That it was a defeat has to be accepted, but from the Scots' point of view it was not sufficiently large or humbling so as to discredit Wallace, the general commanding. It would do the Scots' cause no good to send the general associated with an incompetent performance and comprehensive defeat as their ambassador.

In Wallace's day the connection to Northern Europe was strong, with good weather the Low Countries or Norway was only a few days sailing away. This connection had five strands: trade, immigration, the church, political issues (dynastic affairs by another name) and noble family connections.

Scotland's great nobles have sometimes been presented as an international class or at least a French speaking super-class with the implication that this identity came before their Scottish one. Perhaps, this was true for some, and King John is sometimes mentioned as a strong example. However, this was always much more true of England than Scotland, following the virtual erasure of the ethnic English aristocracy in the decade after Hastings. And although many of the more powerful Scottish noble families did indeed have an international dimension in their connections, for the most part these were historical things; still it added to the familiarity of Europe and Scandinavia to people's world of reference.

Scottish kings and churchmen had long encouraged recruitment of specialist foreign workers in administration, building crafts and manufacturing trades, especially textiles. These added to the natural mix of Scottish society and were regularly topped up as required or when opportunities occurred. Merchants and their associates came and went, sometimes cementing links by marriage, as did the great nobles too. Some of Scotland's foreign visitors would have had connections to the noble families, and this connection would of course run two ways. In this age before mass rapid transit and tourists, Scotland was not, of course, full of foreign visitors. And the connections we speak of are more an east coast phenomenon, diluting as one journeys west and north into the insular mountains; but the point of this is to show that going abroad was not like journeying into a hostile unknown. Scotland, in the age before a British identity, was most firmly within the European orbit. And Wallace must have also thought of himself as a European too, possibly in similar loose manner to that still commonly understood.

Of course, he would have been excited at the prospect of visiting (perhaps again?) the cultural centre of his world and seeing the large and prosperous cities he would have heard merchants and bishops speak of since the days of his childhood. He would have seen riches that would have made his eyes pop. Scotland then had no near equivalent by a very wide margin to Bruges or Rouen or Paris, and visiting these places, and seeing their wealth, and too the agrarian wealth he would have passed through, must have made him realise how small a player in the European scene Scotland was. Perhaps this depressed him a little. Most people have a fair conceit of their own country which a journey abroad can sometimes shake a little.

As a fact, we do not know what he did on this mission. Could he have went to King John, and if so with what purpose or proposal? Surely, such a visit was seriously considered. Regardless of how much the use of his name was a convention or even expedient for some, the war in Scotland was conducted in the King John's name. Yet we do not know the ex-king's take on what was happening. Certainly, the years around the turn of the century were ones of some hope for King John, or at least his line; a sympathetic pope, an ally in France, King Edward's French focus, a fairly united Scottish front, these all argued for the possibility of a deal. Given the presence of English spies and the difficulties of communication, probably only a face to face between the ex king and his greatest champion could provide the crucial answers. Such a meeting would naturally be secret, and thus lost to history. It is fascinating to consider this question with no actual answer, although possibly a tacit one revealed through the silence.

As a fact, though, Wallace would have met princes and barons and bishops. He would have been feted by his hosts as a true and loyal servant to his king, and the man who had defeated the English king's army; this latter especially appreciated by King Edward's enemies and secret ill-wishers. He would have been treated with the greatest of sympathy and respect. But, at the same time, there was always the danger of the assassin's dagger, or treacherous host seeking favour or reward from King Edward. A dagger at midnight saves an army at dawn, this famous truth was well practised in the middle ages. Of all people, Wallace did not need reminded of this and it would have added a hard edge to his trip.

And, worst of all, he would have found when all the kind words were done, it all counted for nothing. Scotland would have to struggle on pretty much alone. The French would help, but only when it suited them. This is not to say that they were insincere in their desire to help Scotland, but they too were faced with a war against England. The reality was that Scotland was just a pawn in the struggle between England and France. And might be saved or sacrificed as it suited. Diplomatic solutions, as they still are, are only viable after all the military ones are exhausted. The talks are just talk.

Wallace would have come back home a wiser man. And too, as encounters with reality often have this effect, a little sadder. He knew now that there was no way of ending the war except by grimly fighting on and on and on. Gradually grinding down the English, if not King Edward's, desire to hold Scotland. King Edward would die, perhaps the new king might not have the same priorities. Those who knew, at least by repute, King Edward's heir, probably sensed this as true. But to ensure this possibility, in the interim more blood would have to be spilt. It was a war in which everyone would lose. And that's how Scotland would win.

Wallace might have returned by the summer of 1301 and taken part in Bruce's campaign to clear the English from South-West Scotland (essentially his own lands). He might have taken part in the Battle of Roslin, in February 1303, in which a large English mounted force of unknown number, perhaps even a few thousand, was surprised and sorely punished by the Scots. But the first definite knowledge we have of his presence in Scotland is in June 1303, when with de Mowbray and Simon Fraser he took part in a campaign in South-West Scotland and over the border into Cumberland. This was intended to force the English to divert troops from their own campaign in central Scotland and send them to defend those areas. It did not work and King Edward had his most successful campaign ever. It looked as if Scotland was done.

In the five years since the defeat at Falkirk, the Scots had continued the fight bravely and in countless small, ugly and forgotten encounters they had matched their foe. There was a shifting cast of Guardians in this period, perhaps due to the desire to spread and share the power, or perhaps because no-one really wanted the job, or could cope with it for long. No set of Guardians, however, were able to build any momentum for their cause. With the failure to get their king back, and the absence of solid support from abroad, there was a gradual but inevitable breakdown of unity over leadership and direction. They were running out of steam. Perhaps, Scotland was just too small to win against a country as mighty as England. Everyone must have thought this, Scot and English, but the ending depended on the Scots accepting it. Increasingly, they were. Although quietly.

And then, at this weak point, a massive blow. Following their crushing defeat at Courtrai against the Flemish in June, 1302, the French were at their own weak point. Their baronial class had been decimated in the battle and the country was in no fit condition to continue the war against England and Flanders. They were obliged to seek peace. The French could not protect Scotland in this situation, although they desired and tried to do so. Nevertheless, in May, 1303, the English and French signed a peace treaty, the Treaty of Paris. King Edward got Gascony back. And the Scots were truly abandoned in their fight now. The English king would bring back from France his best and now even more experienced soldiers, experienced mercenaries would be available and, freed of his French expenditure, more funds would be available for the next Scottish campaign. Scotland would be crushed. The Scots nobles now knew that decision time had absolutely arrived. They either surrendered or would lose everything. King Edward would have Scotland in either case. Choose?

There were no real choices anymore, except for the type of man that embraces destruction. There is such a type whose pride takes him up the gallows step, when it could be avoided by a tactical shift of opinion. Wallace was clearly such a man. Obstinate or principled; actually, probably both. However, most people chose life and made peace with the victor.

King Edward overwintered in Scotland as the end approached for the rebels. His royal presence guaranteeing direct authority to any deals and indicating how seriously he felt about the need for a final solution. That same presence containing the threat of direct military action. If another season of war was necessary, well then, he was already armed and in the enemy's camp. There would be no grace period for continuing rebels, who traditionally would not expect the king's host until late spring at the earliest. He could be at their doors all winter should he choose.

A general surrender was finally agreed on 9th February, 1304. Even the stalwart Comyn family surrendered. King Edward had Scotland in his hand when he held the signed document. Those who refused to surrender or did not (being abroad, for example) were declared traitors. And here we have a list of the noble obstinate; James Stewart, Ingram de Umphraville, Lindsay, de Soules, William Oliphant, the Governor of Stirling Castle held for King John, Simon Fraser. Bishop Wishart was sent to exile, only his cloth of office saving him from a harder fate. But chief of the traitors in the king's book, William Wallace.

THE HARD YEAR

If ever Wallace needed courage it was now.

————◆————

With all around you, even strongest friends, capitulating or dead, it would take an iron will to hang on to your beliefs. Wallace was such a man. Like his adversary, King Edward, he was the sort to keep going until his story ended. This was a time to be flexible, to nod your head and smile and keep your plans in the dark. This was now the time of the shrewd operator, the schemer, the psychologists in this game. Wallace had too much pride to do this. He was part of a long tradition in warrior societies of choosing death before dishonour. Many would regard this as pig-headed, perhaps fanatic even. It is not difficult to accept that this point of view is a valid one.

Wallace was a kind of 'yesterday's man' now. He would still have had a bit of a power base, his special supporters, the common people, many in the church, but with the new peace plan in place the real power shifted to those who made the necessary accommodations. And this was the nobles. It was clear that King John's hopes of regaining the Scottish throne were finished and that the rebellions connected with this phase were also finished. But with this new clarity a question arises: If the Scots were to continue fighting, what were they fighting for? If not to have their own king returned, then what? No-one had an easy answer to this. Other ideas that we may entertain as moderns about what a rebellion could achieve were unknown and unconscionable in those times. A country had to have a king; the reality was now that it was King Edward of England.

We now know, as King Edward did not, that as with his earlier conquest of 1296, the nobles' surrender was tactical and dishonest. Secret plans were definitely in the pipeline, but waiting on the right moment whenever that would be; but certainly, after King Edward's death.

Wallace is our great patriot, but that does not mean that he was always right or that everyone had to agree with him. There comes a time for all leaders when they are rejected. Wallace was no exception. The qualities that made him great were now impediments. Times change. The hard man, the iron will, the inspiring leader of 1297 was not the right leader for the flexible times that followed the surrender. Wallace was not a flexible man.

Now a wanted outlaw with a price on his head, above all the other 'rebels' King Edward wanted Wallace. This desire was powerfully transmitted. Former friends were turned against him, or held to ransom for his capture. Sheriff's officers and bounty hunters would be everywhere. Any who harboured Wallace, or were complicit in allowing him to rest or pass through their jurisdictions, would understand the consequences that would befall them if King Edward found out.

And it would be a simple enough matter to have intelligence of the coming and goings at the homes of Wallace's high profile friends and relatives. Wallace of course knew this, which made meeting or staying with them a doubly risky choice, for it was not just his own life which was being compromised. Wallace just turning up for his dinner would be a quick way to lose friends and family.

By late 1304, this pressure racked up. At Happrew, near Peebles, in February 1304, he and Simon Fraser had a close escape from the English net, although his accompanying force of probably many hundreds was heavily defeated. Another, possibly similar sort of defeat occurred in September at a named but now unknown location which could be in either in Perthshire, Angus or Fife. This has come to be known as the Skirmish of Earnside. Almost nothing is known of this beyond the fact that Wallace escaped, and surely some, if not many, of his reduced force (since Happrew) did not.

This highlights a new problem for Wallace, Fraser and any other rebels; commanding a fairly large force would only serve to draw attention to themselves. And after Earnside, even a small band, say, of a dozen, would do the same. It would be obvious to anyone what they were; after all, what could a group of heavily armed, and surely suspiciously behaving, men pretend to be? No matter how many were sympathetic to them, it would only take one spy in 1,000 to expose them.

Wallace would best then stay free by travelling with a few companions. And staying (or rather, hiding) with lower profile friends, or friends of friends, but sometimes (needs must) he must have had to live rough; again! This would be the time where his hand was always on his dagger. Wallace must have had many close escapes from capture or assassination. Perhaps some would have not lived to rue the day they set out with the intent of having his head.

What was he doing during this period? Was he simply running like a hounded stag with no thought for anything but survival? Wallace could have used his connections to escape abroad, certainly during the sailing season. These same connections, added to his prestige, could easily have found him employment, or at least asylum, in some princely household. He could even, if he wished or for the sake of discretion, have fled abroad in anonymity; then finding employ as a mercenary captain in the retinue of some baron. He could have lain low until the heat died down, or something changed in Scotland that required his presence again; why didn't he?

I believe that this indicates that he still had work to do in Scotland, or felt that he did. But as what? Was he in the background scheming or trying to? Was he trying to persuade people about something, or perhaps they were trying to persuade him? Was he still for King John, or had he accepted that it was time for someone else to take the crown? And although subsequent events showed that Scotland's will for freedom was still strong and that scheming against the English peace was going on, we shall never know if and to what extent Wallace was a part of this. All we know is that the scheming among the Scots nobles was as much directed to themselves as to King Edward. The distrust and accusations that were always present in baronial society, and especially Scotland, were now driven underground by the peace.

This was the climate that Wallace was moving in by summer 1305. Every place a trap, everyone a potential traitor, around every corner an ambush. With all the disappointments it is easy to accept that paranoia and bitterness must have hung around him, and he must not have been easy company. Perhaps, dangerously so. It must have been an emotionally as well as physically tired Wallace that was finally captured at Robroystoun, near Glasgow, on 3rd August, 1305. He was apparently with a woman at the time of capture, described as his 'leman'; perhaps his lover or a harlot. We do not know why he was there, or if he was with companions; if he was they either escaped or were dispatched on the spot. He carried documents whose contents (aside from safe conduct letters from the ex-Scottish, French, Norwegian kings) are unknown. It is sometimes the case that fugitives welcome their capture as a sort of release from the misery of being hunted. This could very well have been Wallace's mind-set. The inevitable had happened; our own age would call it closure.

To prevent any rescue attempt he was immediately whisked to London arriving on 22nd August; a fast journey for those times. Old soldier, Sir John Segrave, the commander of the speedy escort, receiving a substantial fee of 15 shillings (75p) for his efforts. There is the possibility that the haste attendant on his journey to his execution was the result of a desire to have him in London in time to be the main attraction at the Saint Bart's Fair on the 24th of the month. The fair took place at Smithfield, where the execution would take place. Saint Bartholomew was flayed alive; and the fair revellers would have been well aware of the special appropriateness of Wallace's execution then, him being notorious for flaying Cressingham after the battle at Stirling Bridge. It would have seemed to them a punishment most condign and would have added to the pleasure our medieval ancestors enjoyed at such public displays of official cruelty.

The day after arriving he was taken to trial where he heard a list of his crimes against England and the English king read out. The trial was not a trial as we would understand it, more a sentencing. He was already decided as guilty. In any case, much of the evidence against him, certainly as regards atrocities against England and the English were true, as Wallace would have confirmed.

Willelmole Waleys latrone, proditione puplico, utlagato, inimico et rebellione regis (robber, the people's traitor, outlaw, enemy and rebel to the king)

Wallace's only recorded words during the trial were to forcefully deny that he was a traitor to Scotland or to King Edward, for he had never betrayed the first, nor sworn an oath to the second. These claims of his naturally made no difference. By deposing King John, King Edward legally (after his own laws, of course) superseded and nullified oaths sworn for King John. And Wallace was not legally entitled to an opinion on this, nor could such an opinion be the subject of debate. Medieval society was not democratic in law or habit.

Wallace was told of his fate, the traitor's fate; he would not have been surprised at this. This was a standard punishment for that crime in those days. In a curious and terrible way, this fate was a sort of distinction, for Wallace was not treated as a common criminal and just hanged. It is odd to think, but possibly Wallace revelled in this macabre honour. His enemies, perhaps unwittingly, had recognised his impact and his loyalty to Scotland. His life was forfeit when he was caught; all he could hope for then was that his death could be of some significance to himself. The traitor's death was the proof of this.

He would certainly have heard this cruel judgement with a brave face. He was to be hanged, cut down while alive for disembowelling, then beheaded, after which his body would be cut into quarters (from which comes the phrase 'hung, drawn and quartered'). This excessive punishment which would precede his death was, in fact, precisely calibrated to his crimes; the disembowelling and burning of his entrails, for example, was also regarded as a purifying action for his recorded sacrileges; the bowels being regarded as the loci for sacrilegious behaviour. The quarters (actually the limbs) would be sent to various locations throughout the land as a warning of what happens to rebels and a public display of justice meted. The head would go on a spike at London Bridge. It would soon have the company of his brother in arms, Sir Simon Fraser.

Wallace was dragged through the streets of London on a sledge to the place of execution. Such events were always popular, Wallace's even more so. As the wicked and fierce enemy of the English race, everyone would want to see this monster humbled. This procession was meant as a humiliation and its nature with the laughing and jeering crowds meant there was no possibility of maintaining dignity. If ever he needed his faith and his courage it was now.

Blind Harry tells us that Wallace had a last request; that he be allowed to read his old psalter, his prayer book. This was granted by Clifford, an old English knight and enemy from the wars.

To lat him haiff his Psalter buk in sycht.
He gert a preyst it oppyn befor him hauld

He was executed with his eyes fixed on the book held before him by a priest. What better than God at the end. It is comforting to hope that within all Harry's fictions, this comes from true.

Gud devocioun so was his begynnyng
Conteynd tharwith, and fair was his endyng,
Quhill spech and spreyt at anys all can fayr
To lestand blys, we trow forevermayr.

The chopped off limbs were sent to Scotland. But the warning did not work and, as they so often do, had the opposite effect. The year was not out before Robert the Bruce made himself King of Scots and raised another rebellion. A rebellion that after a generation's worth of campaigns, battles and hardship finally wrestled back Scottish independence, recognised in the Treaty of Norham of 1328.

This was Wallace's victory too. And you reading this!

OUR MAN

The story of Wallace does not end with his execution, for future generations of Scots it was the beginning.

Wallace is our talisman, our inspiration, our necessary martyr. The personification of the good cause; the defence of home against an invader. He is among the best of national heroes, for he is untainted in our minds by faction or compromise. He died holding to his principles and doing the best that could be done. Significantly, he died young enough to prevent the perhaps inevitable slide to tyranny, betrayal or irrelevance that spoils the reputation of many real-life heroes. A proper hero must not live long enough to be the villain of his own story.

He appeals also to the democratic sensibility of our own times, and its various forms in earlier ages. The relatively humble background, the taking of personal risks, the rise by merit and service to a principle greater than self or family, mark him as a man to be admired in any age. It is no coincidence that our great champion of the democratic, Robert Burns, was an admirer of Wallace. This appeal bridges the centuries and is a true thing. We are lucky to have such a simple hero in our national identity.

Perhaps, like coming from a good family, we may not even know how great a gift this is.

The lack of details about his life is frustrating, of course, but this fact does not detract at all, I believe, from the factual immensity of his achievement. Without Wallace, the rebellion may have had more of the flavour of a baron's revolt and would have been crushed as they always are. Wallace turned the rebellion into an expression of national identity which united barons and commons in a way not seen before. And they were; this was no war in which titled toffs sent others to do the dying. The entire social strata of Scotland shared in the misery and glory. And without Wallace, no victory at Stirling Brig, no unity in the face of the defeat at Falkirk, no perseverance against a mighty foe. Wallace was not just fighting for a cause, but also it could be argued, defining it and then forging it into a hard thing. Scotland's will for independence, a diamond that could not be crushed.

Of course, there are other hero patriots, the barons: de Soules, de Umphraville, de Mowbray, Lennox, Stewart, Lindsay, Graham, Simon Fraser, to make just a small selection, whom posterity has cast undeservedly into the shadow of this story. And some, the various Comyn family members, whose family connection to King John, eventually led to their significant role in this story being marginalised and misrepresented to the point of calumny. And, of course, the numberless others lost to history, but bearing our names today. However, often at history's crossroad, the choice of path falls to one man. And that was Wallace. That first choice is always a moral one. It is this that distinguishes Wallace from a bandit chief and makes him what he has become for his country's future.

Wallace's generalship has attracted a fair amount of negative criticism, or perhaps in the absence of any solid evidence, negative speculation would be a better wording. While the victory at Stirling was partly dependent on the failings of his enemy, Wallace still deserves massive credit for the successful preparation, deployment and action of the Scottish army on the day. We can never know though how much of this was dependent on Wallace taking good counsel; if it was so, then wisdom is added to his battlefield portfolio without taking much from his tactical genius.

As for Falkirk, we have already considered some of the limiting factors surrounding Wallace's decisions, but one stands out as crucial to the defeat; and this was the presence of mainly Welsh mercenary longbowmen.* It certainly appears as a serious failing on Wallace's part to have not considered their likely impact and have a contingency plan to prevent his schiltroms from exposure to an arrow storm. In his defence, however, the use of massed archers at Falkirk as a major killing power on the battlefield was a new addition to the English manual of

* From a legal point of view the Welsh soldiers in the king's army were now, albeit reluctantly, his subjects and not, strictly speaking, mercenaries. In every other sense they were mercenaries, and regarded as such by their English comrades in arms. This regard was not positive. And, of course, this feeling was mutual.

arms. Archers being previously used by both the Scots and English as ambushers, skirmishers or for harassment purposes; this later use known as bickering in the Scots language. Wallace could not reasonably have foreseen this new use nor imagined (as we can hardly now) the concentrated killing power that could be contained in such a simple weapon thus deployed. Solutions and strategies readily suggest themselves for neutralising this force (the Scots cavalry being tasked with this on this occasion), but they are not simple matters to apply in battle, as the French were to discover over the next two hundred years. When the tactical deployment of strategies to neutralise the mighty longbowmen were successful, for example, as at the Battle of Patay (French vs English) or Otterburn (Scots vs English), victory followed. When not, as most famously (selected from a very long French list!) at Crecy, Poitiers Verneuil and Agincourt, or Halidon Hill (against the Scots), the English longbow prevailed, and crushing defeat and massive casualties followed.

In conclusion, I believe it is fair to say that the evidence for Wallace's generalship (as opposed to his unquestionable leadership and martial prowess) is positive. And nothing more definite can be added or subtracted from this.

It has also been argued that Wallace was a failure because of the rebellion failing in some obvious key objectives. The latter is a fact, but the former a debate about perspectives. But if Wallace gets the blame, so must he also have the credit where it is due. Consider:

As noted, a small and poor country like Scotland simply could not win in any emphatic and final sense against a country like England, so much more powerful and, at that moment, on the verge of becoming the awesome military machine that would ruin France for the next two centuries. But Scotland persevered, and Wallace has to have some credit for this. And while conceding that he was a transitional figure, it must also be noted that he could not be anything else. He knew this. Although he pushed the cultural and political boundaries of his age, no man can live outside his time. And acknowledging it does not belittle his achievement. Countries in his time were run by kings and queens. Wallace could not create a new social order, nor did he try to set himself up as a tyrant ruler, he could only bridge the gap between the departed King John and the next king. This is what his sense of order and honour bade him do. This was his success. Even though he probably died thinking he had failed in this.

But he had not. It may be that his death was indeed a catalyst for the events that followed soon after and led to the Bruce rebellion. Blind Harry has it so, and our hearts too like to find a connection between them to justify better Wallace's death. But even if this is not the direct case, Wallace still led us from King John to Bruce and this was all his mission ever could be.

Significantly, Bruce took up the mantle left by Wallace, that of his country's freedom, rather than his right to kingship; which would have been the standard baronial self-justification for his actions. Indeed, by the time that Wallace was captured, Bruce had already made a secret pact with Bishop Lamberton, Bishop of Saint Andrews, Scotland's foremost churchman, which contained the understanding that the cause of independence would continue under Bruce. Bruce, then, was no usurper king, mad for his family's ambition, but a champion of his people. Bruce was clear about this, just as Wallace had been. This was not self-ambition, but selfless.

In the dark days it was Wallace who stepped out of the shadow with a belief in his country's right and honour. He showed the Scots, at that crucial time of uncertainty, that resistance was possible and could be successful, if they held together and held their nerve. Hold your nerve, our cause is just, and we will thus prevail: this was the simple and great truth he expressed. His gift to our future.

Wallace, our man. As long as Scotland is still Scotland, Wallace will be with us in our heads and ay true in our hearts.

AUTHOR'S NOTE ON SOURCES

Wallace lived in an age that was largely pre-literate.

———◆———

It is not surprising therefore that his name appears only in a few documents and letters. Added together, this information would scarcely fill a postcard. It contains few facts and nothing personal. What we would want to know about Wallace was either never written down in his time, or was destroyed in the various burnings of later wars with England. And yet, Wallace's story, repeated in hundreds of books and the movie *Braveheart*, is packed full of detail and incident. Where did all these facts come from and how much truth is in them?

The source for most of Wallace's story is a 12,000 line epic poem called *Wallace*. It was composed by Henry the Minstrel, also known as Blind Harry or Blin Hary, around 1470, more than 150 years after Wallace's death. In time, as Harry's *Wallace* became an old work, seemingly close to Wallace's own age, it increasingly came to be taken as an accurate version of his life. Of the many books on Wallace that have been published, nearly all have Harry as their ultimate source. This one too, although in a more limited way.

Critical readers of Harry have surely always been aware that much is fanciful, but Harry's claim to have had access to a narrative written by a friend of Wallace has made it difficult to separate the wheat from the chaff.

It was only with the publication of *Hary's Wallace* by Matthew McDiarmid in 1968 that we were able to see Harry's *Wallace* in its true light; a full-bloodied nationalistic, action-adventure story. It is unlikely that Harry had access to any more concrete information on Wallace than we have now. The 'friend manuscript' is a literary fiction, well used in the history of literature. Certainly, Harry would have been able to draw on the story-telling and song tradition for extra tales about Wallace, but no story gains more in the telling than a war story. McDiarmid's brilliant scholarship shows that where Harry's version can be checked against facts it is false, and that the other details in his tale follow narrative conventions of the day and cannot be considered true. Harry's *Wallace* is simply a creation of the imagination. As such, his poem should be considered as a 15th century equivalent of an action movie in the *Die Hard* tradition. Its purpose was entertainment.

But Harry had a serious purpose too. It was to remind the Scots of their proud national pedigree. And, as part of this intention, to restore Wallace to his rightful place in their hearts. His work gives voice to our heartfelt need for a hero. And our need to remember who we are; a need echoed in the popular reaction to the movie, *Braveheart*.

Over the centuries, Blind Harry and Mel Gibson can join hands in agreeing that it is the spirit of the man that matters. I put my hand there too.

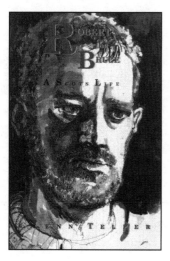